Learning and Living Scripture

an Introduction to the Participatory Study Method

by

Geoffrey D. Lentz
and
Henry E. Neufeld

Energion Publications
P. O. Box 841
Gonzalez, FL 32560
www.energionpubs.com

Energion Publications
P. O. Box 841
Gonzalez, FL 32560

Scripture quotations marked CEV are taken from the **Contemporary English Version**, Copyright © 1995 American Bible Society. Used by permission.

Scripture quotations marked NRSV are taken from the New Revised Standard Version Bible, copyright © 1989 by the Division of Christian Education of the National Council of the Churches of Christ in the U. S. A. Used by permission. All rights reserved.

All other scriptures were translated by Henry Neufeld for this volume.

Cover Design: Jeb Hunt, baxterselite.com.

ISBN10: 1-893729-36-2
ISBN13: 978-1-893729-36-0

Library of Congress Control Number: 2010923156

Copyright © 2010, Geoffrey D. Lentz and Henry E. Neufeld

To our wives

Liz and Jody

who pray while we ceaselessly search
for better methods of Bible study.

The Participatory Study Series

The Participatory Study Series from *Energion Publications* is designed to invite people who wish to study the Bible to become a part of the community of faith that produced the texts we now have as scripture by studying them empathetically and with an aim to learn and grow spiritually.

The section *Using this Book* and the appendices are designed for the series and adapted to the particular study guide. Each author is free to emphasize different resources in the study, and individual students, group leaders, and teachers are encouraged to enhance their study through the use of additional resources.

It is our prayer at *Energion Publications* that each study guide will lead you deeper into scripture and more importantly closer to the One who inspired it.

– Henry Neufeld, General Editor

How to Use This Book

This book is a basic guide to Bible study. We start by presenting the basic principles of the method. These principles led us to develop this system and many of the exercises we suggest. We hope they will help you as well.

You will also notice that we provide exercises for a number of passages. Don't limit yourself to our suggestions, but do work through them. You can use the same idea on another passage, or create similar exercises for yourself and your study group.

The idea is for you to find your own way to get involved. Be creative. It doesn't hurt to use your imagination as long as you remember what is imagination and what is grounded in the text.

For each lesson, begin by reading the text. (There is one exception, which has special instructions at the beginning of the chapter.) Then choose some exercises. If you are working with a small group, divide the exercises between various members of the group and have each one report the results back to the entire group.

This book is best used in community. You can study it by yourself, but sharing with others is a critical part of this method. If you are studying on your own, find people with whom you can share and discuss.

The first section, LEARNING, should be studied in order. The second section, LIVING, can be studied in any order or you can use it selectively.

For further study we provide a number of additional references in the footnotes. As a follow-up study, you may want to consider working through one of these suggested books or web sites. In these footnotes we have added the ISBN to the standard footnote format to make it easier for you to locate these books via online retail web sites.

There are a few terms in the book that are **bolded** when they first occur. These are terms that are not explained extensively in the text, but are included in the Glossary.

For additional help, please check the Participatory Bible Study web site, www.deepbiblestudy.com. In addition, both co-authors blog, Geoffrey Lentz at www.geoffreylentz.com, and Henry Neufeld at www.deepbiblestudy.net. You will find additional information there on many of the topics in this book, and questions are always welcome in the comments.

We pray that God blesses you, and we believe he will, as you study!

Table of Contents

LEARNING

In this first section you learn how to study and get the most from scripture.

Introducing the basic principles of the Participatory Study Method.

Relating the Participatory Study Method to *Lectio Divina*.

Getting a bird's eye view of this approach to Bible study

Getting ready for study and finding the best resources to aid in your study.

Praying throughout your Bible study time

Learning to read in order to get an overview of the passage and understand the context.

The heart of your study in which you dig deeper and deeper into the text.

Sharing is critical both for living as a witness and for being accountable.

LIVING

In this section, you put into practice what you learned in the first section by studying and sharing passages of scripture from various types of literature found in the Bible.

What types of literature can you find in the Bible and what difference does this make?

Studying Bible stories and learning to apply them in your own life.

Understanding the history of God's action in the world as told in the Bible story and in the many many Bible books that contain history.

Looking at the metaphorical and symbolic language in the Bible.

END MATTER

LEARNING

All scripture is inspired by God ...
2 Timothy 3:16

1

Introduction

Introducing the basic principles of the Participatory Study Method

Most Christians know that studying the Bible is a crucial part of their spiritual development. Many people feel guilty for not studying the scriptures as much as they think they should. We believe this lack of study is largely due to two things. First, many people lack the basic skills, study methods, and organization required to learn scripture. Second, the Bible is a complicated book with many different types of writings that can be read and interpreted in different ways. This book is designed as a guide to help with both of these issues.

You will find a full method for reading scripture and getting the most out of it. You will find references to many study helps including commentaries, Bible dictionaries, concordances, and study editions of the Bible. It can help you find a translation that meets your study needs. The method presented in this book can help you study the Bible privately, as part of a small group, or even lead a group Bible study. This series includes study guides developed on several books of the Bible that use this method.

This book also helps to make the Bible more accessible. Different parts of the Bible must be read in different ways. For instance a Psalm is to be read and interpreted in a different way than a chapter of Mark or Revelation. This book will give you details about many types of writing in the Bible and how to get the most out of reading them.

What is participatory Bible study? Normally we call Bible study participatory when everybody in a group participates. This distinguishes it from those groups in which one person speaks and the rest simply absorb.

In the participatory study method we take that a step further. Not only do you need to personally participate in Bible study, but you need to become part of the Bible story. This may seem like a tall order. Just how can you do that?

If you have become a Christian, you are now part of the Bible story. Participatory Bible study invites you to find your place in the story and live positively according to God's will, doing your part to carry the great drama forward. Are you going to be aware of your role in the greatest drama in history, or will you be passive and just let things happen to you?

Many Bible students get very little from their study. When they do study seriously, they are very dependent on commentators, and they're not sure just how the interpretations are produced. Some get involved in the technical details of Bible study, but then either give up, or become bogged down in hunting down minor points, and miss much of the blessing that is available.

Our conviction is that Bible study should be about experiencing God. It is not just learning *about* God or learning doctrines taught by others. It is about getting a first hand experience of what God has to say to you and then living as one of God's children.

1. The first key is to *get the Bible out from between you and God*. Let God speak to you. Let the Bible help. Don't let the Bible be a barrier.

   The Bible is not the only way you access God. It is not necessarily God's primary way of communicating with you personally. Rather, it provides a light on your own relationship with God. The question is this: How can I

GOD	GOD
↑	↑
BIBLE	BIBLE
	↑
PERSON	PERSON

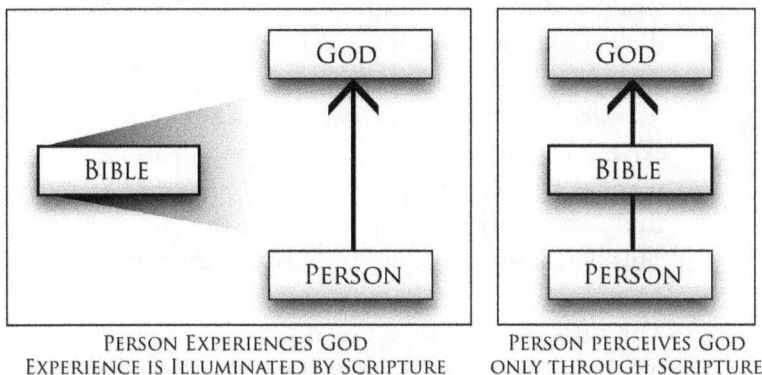

PERSON EXPERIENCES GOD	PERSON PERCEIVES GOD
EXPERIENCE IS ILLUMINATED BY SCRIPTURE	ONLY THROUGH SCRIPTURE

improve my relationship with God through understanding how these other writers related to God?[1]

2. The second key is to *approach the Bible with a desire to learn*, not to find support for what you already know. This seems simple, but in the church we are often so tied up with our doctrinal statements, or more likely weak memories of them, and also so afraid that our own ideas might be *wrong* or that someone will call them (gasp!) *heresy*, that we really can't listen openly to what the Bible says. We're not saying that the Bible is going to overturn all your traditional doctrines. We *are* saying that you should not worry about being wrong as you try to understand what the Bible says, and particularly what God is saying to *you* as you study the Bible.

3. The third key is to make a serious and active effort to *understand just what it was that the people in Biblical times experienced*, and how they responded to it. Get to know them as they were. It's impossible to do this perfectly, but it is worth your effort to do your best. This means accurate and empathetic reading. It also means some humility – not assuming that you are more intelligent,

---

1 For further study on Biblical inspiration, we would recommend Henry Neufeld, *When People Speak for God* (Gonzalez, FL: Energion Publications, 2007. ISBN: 1-893729-38-9).

wiser, more ethical, and have a better imagination than the people you're reading about.

4. The fourth key is to *look at yourself and your spiritual community carefully and honestly*, and try to *bring your experiences together with those of others*. This is how the participation is brought forward to the present and your Bible study starts to impact who you are as a person. This is where you begin not just to *learn* scripture, but to *live* it.

5. The fifth key is to *share your experiences* with others, and to try to translate your understanding so that they can also understand and participate. Don't be afraid to talk about ethical issues without reference to the Bible. If you really understand what you have learned in your Bible study and your communion with God, you should be able to support it on another basis. We believe that if God is the creator of the universe, and we have understood what God wants, it should also be rational to some degree.

Principles Behind the Method

> The Spirit will teach you everything. – *John 14:26 (CEV)*
>
> The people of Berea were much nicer than those in Thessalonica, and they gladly accepted the message. Day after day they studied the Scriptures to see if these things were true. – *Acts 17:11 (CEV)*

A new Bible student quoted John 14:26 to me when she was about to quit my class in basic Bible study. "I don't have any problem with what you are teaching," she said, "but I think the Holy Spirit can teach me all that." Perhaps she needed to follow up by reading about the Bereans in Acts 17!

While I believe that the Holy Spirit is the best teacher, I still believe that this girl needed some of the material in my class. The Holy Spirit tends to teach us through many means; teachers, preachers, prophets, speaking to us directly, taking us through some difficult times of study, and the use of our God-given minds.

The participatory method of Bible study is designed to bring all these different factors together. It asks you to get yourself involved in the experience that the Bible represents, to look for the ways in which the material can apply to you. You don't have to accept everything to use this method, but you do have to be willing to be as empathetic as possible with the characters of the Bible story, and the writers of the Bible books. You have to be willing to try to understand things from their perspective.

If you believe further, as we do, that God is speaking through these experiences and writings, then you will want to go further. After you have understood the principles on which they were basing their lives, you will want to find out what principles God was trying to teach, and then how you can apply those principles directly in your own life, and in the life of your community. If you do that, you can be involved in building the body of Christ in a new and ever growing way.

The Bible presents these principles in ways that may seem strange to you. Sometimes they are contained in rituals. Sometimes they are contained in stories. At other times they may be hidden in allegories or in symbolic visions. Each of these methods communicated some part of God's message to someone. The hidden pearls of God's truths are within a matrix of another person's times, problems, and assumptions – you could say in their entire culture. What we try to do is get at the principles and find a way to apply them in *our* time and culture.

In order to do this, there are some key questions. These questions will be repeated in the chapters on interpreting particular types of literature, because while the interpretive method changes, the final result will often remain the same.

   ◆   What is the experience behind this passage?

- How might the experience reflected in this passage relate to my own experience?
- What principle(s) lies behind the specific statements?
- How might the principles relate to my life?

In order to answer these questions, we have to come to understand the Bible writers, their time and culture as much as possible. Fortunately, we have a great deal of material available right *in* the Bible to help us do that. We can then find out why they did particular things, and learn how to use those principles constructively. It is quite possible for a Bible student to make decisions based on the *mistakes* of some Bible characters or writers. The Bible records their mistakes, often in some detail. But when you understand the passage, why it is there, and what principles it conveys, then you can make use of it in a practical and helpful way.

There is no shortcut in Bible study. If you want to find what God has for you in scripture, you will have to dig. There are some things you can do to make your study time more profitable. The participatory method is not going to be easier than other methods of inductive Bible study. It is our aim, however, that it be more practical, with the focus always on learning how we can become better disciples of Jesus.

2

Reading with God

Relating the Participatory Study Method to Lectio Divina.

The key principle of this study method is that the Bible should not be read like other books. It was intended to be read with God in mind. The goal of Bible study is not primarily more information about God but more formation in the way that God wants you to be.

Lectio divina, which means holy reading, is an ancient practice of studying scripture. It has been done in many ways since Origen described it around 220 AD. The great monastic traditions of the church further developed it into distinct phases and practices. The basic principle is that reading and studying the Bible should be remarkably different than reading the morning paper or studying Shakespeare. The Bible is a sacred text; it is a *Living Word*. It should not be studied like it is dead pages from history.

Lectio Divina is a practice that, through the power of the Holy Spirit, invites the risen Christ to interpret scripture to us anew. It is a prayerful reading of scripture that expects God to speak once again through his Holy Word. Prayer should influence the way you study the Bible, and studying the Bible should influence the way you pray. In *lectio divina*, it is impossible to tell when you are studying and when you are praying. There is no difference.

This practice is usually applied on small passages of scripture for an extended period of time. However, in the participatory study method, practices similar to those of *lectio divina* are used as a strategy to study as much as an entire book of the Bible. This is somewhat challenging because the scripture text is so large, but the prayerful approach is still crucial to Christian study of the scripture. In these lessons, the ancient practice of *lectio* is blended with modern study methods that takes into account the historical, cultural, and literary contexts.

The historical methods are important to us because they help connect us to people of a different time and place who experienced the same God that we do, learned from the same texts, and were led by the same Spirit. We do not study history because we think history *is* the meaning; we study history to help us meet those who wrote the texts and those who have studied the passages before us.

The four moments of *lectio divina* established by Guigo II, a 12th century Carthusian monk, in a book called *The Monk's Ladder*. He organized the practice around four rungs that help us draw closer to God through reading the Bible.

Reading (*lectio*): The first rung of the ladder is reading. Believe it or not, this is the step most often skipped or diminished. It is important to do the Bible reading for each exercise, or each passage in your own study, in order to get the most out of it. Ideally it should be read several times so that you can become familiar with the language and themes of the text. This book is a guide to help you study the Bible. It is a supplement to the Biblical text; the text itself should have primary focus in your study. The steps of the participatory study method emphasize different ways of reading to help the text become part of you as you study.

Meditating (*meditatio*): The next thing to do is to prayerfully meditate on the text. Dig deep into it. Study the words. Break it down into pieces. Most of the activities in chapter seven (The Central Loop) are part of *meditatio*. Look up words to find their meaning. Notice if there are any words or actions that the Holy Spirit may be leading you to examine further.

Praying (*oratio*): Third, we learn to pray the text. Use what you have learned from the scripture to formulate a prayer. It may be helpful to write it down. This is where the text really becomes alive to us.

In the participatory study method, prayer is not seen as simply one part of the study; prayer permeates your study. You start with prayer and listening so that you will hear what God has to say through the text. Then you turn what you have heard from God back into prayer. The prayer (or conversation with God) never ceases!

Contemplating (*contemplatio*): The last step is the most difficult and rewarding. You have *read* the text, *studied* the text, *prayed* the text. Now it is time to *be* the text. Let it seep into your being. Be still and listen. Make sure you leave some time after the prayer for silence and reflection. It is said that Dan Rather once interviewed Mother Theresa about her prayer life. Rather asked her, "What do you say to God when you pray?". Her answer was simple; "I don't say anything; I just listen." After that he asked, "Well, what does Jesus say to you?" And Mother Theresa answered, "Oh, He doesn't say anything, either. He just listens." Listening is what is important. You may not always feel anything, but God is there.

Another facet of contemplation is to learn to *do* the text. We cannot be just hearers of the word, we must also be doers of the word. Let the scripture change the way you live your life.

Exercise

Choose a short passage of scripture and try to apply the four step method described in this chapter. If in a group, you should probably choose one of these familiar passages.

- Psalm 23
- Matthew 5:1-20
- John 1:1-18

3

Overview of the Method

Getting a bird's eye view of this approach to Bible study

Now that we have discussed the understanding of scripture and the basic ideas that lie behind this method, we need to get down to the nuts and bolts. We have reduced the participatory study method to a simple set of steps.

These steps are a way to get started. For example, we list prayer as a step, but prayer should be part of your Bible study from start to finish. As you become more familiar with the Bible and with this approach to study you will also develop your own style.

But for now, just to get started, follow this simple outline.

> ➤ Preparation
>
> ➤ Prayer
>
> ➤ Overview
>
> ➤ The Central Loop
>
>   ◦ Study the Background
>
>   ◦ Meditate
>
>   ◦ Question
>
>   ◦ Research
>
>   ◦ Compare
>
> ➤ Share

We will give a brief description of each of these elements, and then the each of the following chapters will cover one of the major points.

Preparation

As you begin the study, preparation will involve getting the materials you want to use, choosing your passage of scripture, and making decisions about the time and resources you can devote to this study.

Prayer

This is also your time of prayer. Before you begin to read, you need to pray. As part of your prayer, you need to listen. You come to the text because God calls you to it. Pray specifically for an open mind to understand, an open heart to receive, and enabling grace for the actions you will need to take.

We emphasize prayer *before* Bible study, but it should also be an ongoing part of your study from start to finish, and should continue as you go on to live the text.

Overview

Getting a quick overview is accomplished by reading a passage through at least once, but preferably three times, and in exceptional cases up to 12 times. Don't feel bad about how many times you read. Choose a number that seems reasonable to you. If you start reading the third time, and it feels like a burden, move on. This is part of *lectio* but only a part. You will learn to read in other ways in different phases of your study.

Once you have read the passage through several times, read one or two of the following :

1. The entry on the book of the Bible in which your passage occurs in a Bible handbook, such as Zondervan's

2. The entry on the book of the Bible in a Bible dictionary.

3. The introductory note on that book or section in your study Bible. Many study Bibles include introductions to subsections of the Bible books. These can be very helpful when studying a short passage, but you will normally need to read the introduction to the whole book first.

4. The introductory section of a good commentary on the book.

Here is where we introduce historical elements into your study. Don't imagine that God cannot talk to you through this text because you are so far separated from the people who wrote it. They were people like you who had hopes, dreams, gifts, and failings. Study the background to help you connect to them. Christianity is a community that includes those who have gone before us in the communion of the saints.

The Central Loop

The central loop is the deeper study, often repeated in many ways, of your chosen passages.

It is most closely related to *meditatio*, but the implementation of *meditatio* also includes questioning the text in a directed way. Don't concentrate on the boundaries between one activity and the next. They are all related!

With each topic there will be an opportunity to try to think of new questions one might ask for further study. Generating new questions keeps us from getting stale. Not only do we not have all the answers; we don't even have all the questions!

Think of a question primarily as a way to prepare your mind to hear the text. When we listen or read, we often hear what we expect to hear. If we're listening to the radio for weather, we may miss a major discussion of politics. You can miss what God is saying to you through a Bible writer because you are looking for something else. Questioning is thus an important part of *meditatio*, but it also relates closely to *oratio*. Take your questions to God in prayer.

Sharing

The final step is sharing. You do this both to give others the benefit of what you have learned and to benefit from their comments and perhaps corrections.

As you study and question, find something to share. Remember that sharing can be in the form of a question. For example, one might ask others how they understand a particular word, such as "incarnation," "poverty," or "atonement." Take notes on their answers, and bring that information back to your study.

Then ask yourself what your neighbors will hear when you make particular statements, such as "I must be bold for Jesus!" or "Jesus is the only way to receive atonement." Do those statements mean something to them? Do they mean the same thing to them as they do to you?

This is part of *contemplatio*, as you try to *be* and *do* the text. We often think of sharing primarily as telling someone things that we have learned. But if what you learned is that God loves prisoners, for example, you might find that the best way of sharing that lesson is to become active in prison ministry.

Sharing demonstrates that you don't believe the text is your private possession. It is God's gift to the Christian community.

Exercise

1. Read Psalm 19 aloud.

2. Meditate on certain words or phrases that stick out in your mind (e.g. *making wise the simple, the fear of the Lord is pure*, or *acceptable*). Repeat them several time aloud or

privately. You can also look a word up in a Bible dictionary, Bible cross reference, or concordance.

3. Try to build a prayer that uses the language of the scripture. Examples: "May the words of my mouth and the meditations of my heart be acceptable to you," or "God, open my eyes to see all that the heaven are telling me of your glory."

4. Sit in silence for a few minutes. Think about what God is trying to tell you through this text. How might this text apply to what is going on in your life? Do you feel that God's instructions are sweeter than honey? Sit in God's presence and be open to the Holy Spirit.

4

Preparation and Resources

Getting ready for study and finding the best resources to aid in your study

Preparation

I was in a Bible study group in which we were discussing the gospels. We had just read one of the many passages in which the disciples fail to understand something that Jesus was teaching them. One class member immediately responded, "How could the disciples be so stupid? How could they possibly not understand?"

This type of response is very common in Bible study groups. We look at the Bible stories from outside, from the perspective of advanced, better informed people who obviously know much better than those who were involved. When we look from that perspective, we will tend to find the things in the story that will help us justify ourselves. "We are better; they were worse. We have advanced so much since their time!"

We're not suggesting that we need to behave precisely as the characters in Bible stories behaved. What we *are* suggesting is that we need to come to the Bible prepared to learn from the text as we read it. We can learn from the good and the bad, from the clear and from the unclear. Having a learning attitude, and allowing our thinking to be challenged is more important than simply learning the facts.

In order to do this we need to be prepared for the type of study we plan to do, and also to be prepared in terms of our attitude. This is why we emphasize prayer before and during Bible study, or for those who are just looking at the Bible, but are not Christians, we recommend thinking specifically about your attitude as you study. This does not mean that you must decide to agree with everything that you read. Rather, you decide to learn from their experiences, and judge their experiences from their perspective.

Types of Study and their Purpose

We can place types of study along a continuum from general light reading to serious, point by point study. Don't get the idea from the word "light" or "serious" that we think one end of the spectrum is better than the other. We think Bible study needs to involve a variety of activities, from reading long passages quickly, to careful examination of every grammatical detail of a verse.

Your preparation will relate to what you're trying to do. When you set out to do some light reading of lengthy passages, select an easy to read Bible version and sit down in a place that is comfortable for you and just read. You don't have to concentrate constantly in this case; the process is very similar to that of reading a novel. This will allow you to get an overview of whole books or blocks of books. For example, you can read Luke and Acts together in this way, trying to complete both books at one sitting. Other large blocks are Joshua through Kings, Chronicles along with Ezra and Nehemiah, or the entire Pentateuch (or just the narrative portions of it). Just remember to prepare for the type of study you intend to do.

Choosing a Passage

Your approach to study is going to depend on what you're trying to study. You may be wondering just how you select the passage you're going to study.

It may be that you have a passage selected for you, such as in your Sunday School curriculum, your church bulletin with the scripture reading on Sunday morning, or the passage selected by your small group.

If you are looking for a place to start there are a number of options.

1. **Reading the Bible through.** Many people try this method first, but it isn't one of the better approaches to Bible study. You tend to get some of the most difficult material to interpret early in your study, such as Leviticus and Numbers.

2. **Choosing a Bible book.** Mark or John are good books to start with, though you'll want to return to John again when you have more experience. John is simple on one level, but it offers depths that can only be reached through long and careful study.

3. **Choosing a topic.** This isn't an approach we recommend in general, but if you study substantial passages from various books on a subject it can be valuable.

4. **Using the Lectionary.** The Lectionary is a calendar of Bible readings selected for use during the Christian year. These normally include an Old Testament passage, a Psalm, a selection from one of the epistles, and a gospel reading. The Lectionary uses three cycles of readings, each covering one year, cycles A, B, and C. You can find the current readings at www.textweek.com. If your church uses a Lectionary for worship, studying the Lectionary each week may help deepen your worship experience and further your learning.

Materials

Each person will use different materials. There are three major elements in deciding what materials you will use:

1. **Notes**

If you like to take notes, you may want some extra note paper. Look for a size of paper that is easy to use, and also easy to preserve and organize. Pens or pencils for notes can be of any color you choose. Many Bible students use different colored pens in underlining, and occasionally in note taking, with the various colors indicating particular subjects. Some people don't find that color coding helps them a great deal, but don't hesitate to invest in some pens if it does.

I tend to keep my notes in the margins of my Bible. As one of my wedding presents I received a New Revised Standard Version, printed by Cambridge University Press in their wide margin Minster text. I can take notes in the margins and add cross-references. I even keep complete sermon notes in the margins simply by giving my next scripture reference along with each key point.

Recently, I have started to keep many of my notes in my Logos Bible software, which keeps them organized, and prevents me from discarding scraps of paper that have crucial notes.

The bottom line here is to do what works, both in terms of colors and where you keep your notes.

2. **Underlining**

Again, there are different approaches. Some readers tend simply to underline key points in the author's development of his idea. I find using a highlighters with a colored flag dispenser attached helpful to tap items for follow up study. Highlighters and/or colored pens can make it easy to track down materials on a particular subject. Again, there are no rules here, but get the materials you need to mark texts and keep the notes you want for your study.

3. **Purpose of your Study**

   Consider the purpose of your study. There are several places in in this text where we suggest reading large portions of scripture quickly in order to get an overview. If you are going to sit down to read quickly, you may need nothing other than your Bible and a place to sit. If you are reading for an overview, resist the temptation to underline or take notes. As you read quickly, try to take in the whole picture.

Here are some possible materials and how they would be used.

- **Pen**
  Note taking, including marginal notes if your Bible allows
- **Colored pens or highlighters**
  Mark passages according to topic
- **Good study location, desk, lighting**
  Make yourself comfortable while you study
- **Music or other background sound**
  Some people like to study with praise music running
- **Notebook**
  If you prefer to take notes somewhere other than your margin
- **Computer**
  Allows you to use Bible study software or to take notes
- **Devotional guides**
  If you have trouble deciding where to start

Attitude Preparation

Your attitude preparation is really very simple. Get ready to listen and discern, but not to condemn. You are going to be reading about people who lived in a culture very different from your own.

Reading with an open mind doesn't mean that you accept everything that the characters or even the writers say and do. You don't have to view their culture as the ideal. What you do need to do is understand their actions within the limits of what they knew and within their circumstances. It's very easy to assume that someone should have known better when you don't understand their situation.

For example, much of the violence in the Bible needs to be understood in the context of the times. We're not going to try to resolve all of the issues that result from incidents of violence in the Bible in this book, but we would like to suggest some ideas that must be a part of understanding violent passages.[2] Christians have often reacted in one of two extreme ways. Some would reject all of those passages by rejecting the entire Old Testament, claiming it is superseded by the New. That does eliminate many difficult passages, but it both leaves some unresolved issues with the New Testament, and it tends to cut off a large percentage of the way in which God has worked with people. On the other hand, some Christians use violent passages in the Bible to justify being violent people now; if the Israelites could make war and wipe out whole cities, we are justified in advocating the same thing. If the Israelites stoned people to death, we can do the same.

It looks as though God's message in the Bible had to be targeted at the situation in which people lived. Reform is not as easy to implement as we may think. Thus one needs to understand people's violent actions in the context of a violent world. At the same time, one cannot justify actions now based on the situation then. The question for a Christian would be, what direction is

---

2   For a more in-depth discussion of violent passages in the Bible see Alden Thompson, *Who's Afraid of the Old Testament God?* (Gonzalez, FL: Energion Publications, 2004, ISBN: 1-893729-07-9).

Jesus leading us? Is Jesus calling us to violence or to more peaceful action? This can be a complex question, but is part of the joy of Bible study.

First, learn to understand what people did and why in their context, then as you study you may be able to learn what God was trying to do with them, and by extension what God is trying to do in your own life.

Resources

Get a small, well-selected set of study materials. Critical resources for study include:

Bibles

It is usually valuable to have two or three translations available, one for fast reading, one for more serious study, and one for comparison. For more information on selecting Bible translations, *What's in a Version?*[3] (pamphlet) or the *Energion Publications* book[4] by the same name.

Some suggestions for a list of three translations are:

Reading	Study	Comparison
Contemporary English Version	New Revised Standard Version	New Living Translation
New Century Version	English Standard Version	Revised English Bible
New Living Translation	New American Standard Bible	The Message

You need one Bible that is very easy for you to read. You'll use that one for rapid reading or reading of long passages or whole books of the Bible. This will usually be a translation using

---

3 Energion Publications, Participatory Study Series Pamphlets, General Catalog, http://catalog.participatorystudyseries.com.
4 Henry Neufeld, *What's in a Version?* (Gonzalez, FL: Energion Publications, 2004 ISBN: 1-893729-20-6).

functional equivalence, which is a more idiomatic style of translation. The first column in the chart above lists such translations.

Choose a second translation that uses **formal equivalence** to allow you to work with concordances better. Formal equivalent translations tend to me more consistent in translating the same Greek or Hebrew word with a single English word.

Finally, choose one translation that comes from a different tradition than your own.. Protestants might want to use a Catholic Bible such as the New American Bible or New Jerusalem Bible, and Catholics might want to choose an evangelical Bible such as the New Living Translation.[5]

Concordances

You will want a good concordance to at least one of your versions. In early study, a concordance in the back of your Bible may be adequate, but later you will want a larger concordance, or some good Bible study software to allow you to do topical and word searches.

Bible Dictionaries and Encyclopedias

If you have some good Bible software you will probably get a selection of these resources, but otherwise, you may want to have one or two on hand. A Bible dictionary will help you get past words that you don't understand.

Study Bibles and Commentaries

We recommend that you use these sparingly in your early study, and let yourself hear what the scriptures say to you. There is one exception – the introductory material to books. Having one of

---

5   You can find out more about various types of translations at Bible Version Selection Tool, http://mybibleversion.com, maintained by Energion Publications.

your Bibles in a study edition will allow you to get historical and background information that won't be available otherwise.

The number of resources you can use may seem overwhelming and can get very expensive. One good collection of resources is your church library. If your library doesn't already have good materials on Bible study, consider working with your church librarian or library committee and try to get some good commentaries and Bible dictionaries, then encourage church members to learn to use them.

Conclusion

Preparation is the most individual element of Bible study. Make sure you have the materials and the mental preparation that will allow you to listen to God as you study.

Exercise

With all of study preparation materials that you choose in front of you, open your Bible up to Psalm 19 .

Use your highlighters to mark key words and make some notes in the margin if you wish. The best margin notes are questions that help open up the text or references to other scriptures. For example, several of our study Bibles say that Roman 1:19-20 is a related text and may help bring fuller understanding to the Psalm.

Look up your highlighted/underlined words in a Bible Dictionary and/or concordance. Read the notes in your study Bible and look up the text in a commentary.

1. Write down (or type) several notes on what you are discovering in study.

2. Look up key words in a Bible dictionary.

3. Look up key words in your concordance.

4. Read the introduction to the Psalms in your study Bible. If there are notes regarding Psalm 19, read those as well.

5. Did you find answers to any of the questions you wrote in your Bible's margins?

6. What new questions did you find while reading?

5

Prayer

Praying throughout your Bible study time

Prayer is the key to making your Bible study into a conversation with God.

As you begin your study, claim these promises:

> But if we confess our sins to God, he can always be trusted to forgive us and take our sins away. – *1 John 1:9 (CEV)*

> I will sprinkle you with clean water, and you will be clean and acceptable to me. I will wash away everything that makes you unclean, and I will remove your disgusting idols. I will take away your stubborn heart and give you a new heart and a desire to be faithful. You will have only pure thoughts, because I will put my Spirit in you and make you eager to obey my laws and teachings. – *Ezekiel 36:25-27 (CEV)*

Attitude

It's quite possible that some who are using this manual are not believers or do not accept some of the underlying theological assumptions on which we base this method.

Even so there is one aspect of prayer that you should apply – the attitude of learning. Think for a few moments about your aim in study, and lay aside any attitudes that would prevent you from understanding. You are looking for the same attitude of mind in that you don't have to approve of what you read, but you will be better off hearing it as much as possible, in the way it was intended. Later, when you compare it to your own life, is the time to accept and/or reject elements based on whether they are valuable to you or not.

Example Prayer for Bible Study

Lord, take from me any thought habits which will keep me from hearing. Make me open to your voice and your voice alone.

Lord, help me to accept your people as my brothers and sisters in your kingdom and let me learn and grow from both their weaknesses and their strengths.

Lord, I trust you to reveal yourself to your people the way you know is best. Let your will be done.

Lord, let me not only recognize but obey your voice. Let my actions be conformed to your will. Help me to love my neighbor as myself.

In Jesus' name, Amen.

Exercise

Choose one of the many prayers in the Bible and try to pray it for yourself or your group. We have suggested praying scripture as part of your general studies. One of the easiest places to try this is with a Bible prayer.

Here are some prayers:

- Matthew 6:9-13
- John 17
- Daniel 9:3-19
- Psalm 138

There are many others. You can try the Energion Prayer Index[6] if you would like more examples. There is also more information on adapting scriptural prayers in the book *I Want to Pray!*.[7]

---

6   Energion.com Prayer Index, http://prayer.energion.com
7   Perry M. Dalton and Henry Neufeld, *I Want to Pray!* (Gonzalez, FL: Energion Publications, 2005, ISBN: 1-893729-31-1), pp. 9-18.

6

Overview

*Learning to read in order to get an overview of the passage
and understand the context*

The overview phase of Bible study is the time for you to get
your bearings. Fix in your mind the key elements of what your
text says and where it is in the Bible story as a whole. As you
continue to study, you will expand and correct this information
and go into more detail, but try not to lose a sense of the whole
passage.

Read the passage multiple times. Twelve or more can be a real
blessing, but any number from three times up will help.
Memorizing is useful, at least of key texts. (This will also require
you to select key texts.) Read from different Bible versions, to
help you with your concentration and to open up different ways
of understanding the passage.

At this point don't use commentaries, study notes, your
concordance, or anything which takes your concentration off of
the passage you are studying.

This is the stage that most people tend to ignore or to spend
very limited time on. If you do spend time on it, you will reap a
reward. The ideal situation is to read the passage enough times
so that you have a clear picture in your mind of the key points or
key events covered by the passage. Reading one thing should
suggest other portions of the book or passage and their
relationship. This can be a daunting task when you are dealing

with whole books of the Bible, especially longer ones, so start with shorter passages.

This reading will form a foundation for a number of exercises that we suggest in the sections on studying particular types of literature in the Bible. Often you will be asked to form a complete picture of the material, tell a version from a different viewpoint, or describe the background.

Overview Reading

Some people may find overview reading difficult or even boring due to repetition. Here are some suggestions for making this type of reading work better.

- **Use multiple translations** – When memorizing, of course, we suggest selecting a single version. But when reading for an overview and to fix the general ideas of a passage in your mind using multiple translations will help you concentrate. It also prevents you from "seeing what you already know is there."
- **Choose passages wisely** – In the early stages, choose a passage that interests you and for which you have the background. If you've never done this before, don't start on Leviticus, for example. The Sermon on the Mount, one of Jesus' sermons in the gospel of John, or even the whole epistle of 1 John are much easier examples.
- **Have a pen and/or marker handy** – Don't get too caught up in notes, but mark things each time and write marginal notes.
- **Follow up promptly** – Follow up your reading by serious, line by line study of the passage without too much delay.
- **Allow yourself enough time** – If you are reading a chapter, you probably need to do this over several days. (For memorizing, you want to do this as quickly as possible. For study, allow yourself time to think and

meditate.) For a whole book, you might allow yourself several weeks.

- **Don't neglect prayer** – Always study prayerfully and with time for meditation and listening for the Holy Spirit to apply the passage to your own life.

The foundation of Bible Study is reading the text, and yet this is the step that most people spend the least amount of time on or skip all together. Reading the whole text several times to gain an overview will be greatly beneficial for deeper Bible study.

Exercise

Take one of the following passages and read it at least three times:

1. The Sermon on the Mount (Matthew 5-7)
2. The Story of the Creation and Fall (Genesis 1-3)
3. The Prayer of Jesus (John 17)
4. 1 John
5. Philemon

If you are studying in a small group, try telling the rest of the group what your passage says in your own words. If you are working on your own, try one of the following, which can also be used in the group setting:

1. Write your own version of the passage. For example, you could write a modern style sermon taking up the content of the sermon on the mount.
2. Draw a picture that represents the passage to you.
3. Write a poetic or even a prose response to the passage either as yourself or as a historic person. For example, you could write a response to Philemon as you imagine Philemon might have responded. Alternatively recast the

letter into a similar request from a Christian leader sent to you and respond.

If you are studying on your own, find someone to share the results of your exercise or talk about it over a meal with friends and family.

7

The Central Loop

The heart of your study in which you dig deeper and deeper into the text

We call this the central loop because it is often repeated in studying. You look at the background, identify questions, find some answers, and then generate more questions. Often you have to look back at the background for some of the answers.

How long you continue this study is up to you, based on how deeply you want to delve into a particular passage.

Study the Background

Find out who wrote the passage, to whom it was written, what is the situation being addressed, and what type of literature it is. The background is composed of these four features discovering *who* is writing *to whom*, *why* and *by what method*.

When you first start studying the Bible, this is the one place to use a study Bible or a Bible commentary. Read the introduction to the book and try to get some of the historical background. As you study more, you will probably begin to develop your own ideas about the background of some Bible passages or whole books. A number of the exercises we suggest in discussing how to study specific types of literature involve picturing the background. For example, one can read epistles such as 1 Corinthians or Hebrews, and try to picture the situation of the people to whom the letter was written. Writing a specific description can help you understand the reasons for some of the statements in the book.

Once you have read the background material, you may want to compare and contrast the background of this book with your own situation. Most introductions to 1 Corinthians, for example, will say certain things about the church in Corinth. Ask yourself how your church is similar or different, and record your answers. (See Exercise, p. 49).

Meditate, Question, Research, Compare (Repeat as needed)

Meditate

Meditate on the passage. If you are having difficulty meditating, think about telling someone else about the passage, such as a friend in need of encouragement, someone who is unsaved, or a child. Think: What questions might they ask about this passage? You can formulate thought questions or fact questions. Fact questions are about what the author is actually saying. Thought questions may lead you to other revelations well beyond the intended statement of the passage. In this case your questioning is used to help you understand how someone else might see the passage. In the next section we will discuss formulating various types of questions.

Meditating can take many forms. Often it is a dialog with yourself and with the Holy Spirit as to what the passage means and how it applies to you.

In order to meditate on a passage you have to read it, and read it well enough so that you can think about the words without having them in front of you.

Reading the Text Precisely

Many of us assume that we read texts precisely and comprehend what we read. For the most part, we are probably right, especially when those texts are modern texts written either by people we know (such as letters) or by people who live in a culture similar to ours. When material is highly technical, however, it is important to learn to read more precisely. Such precise reading is a prerequisite to meditating on a text.

Most of the Biblical text was not intended as technical, though certainly things such as the laws of the Torah (Pentateuch) are very technical. But because the Bible is regarded as a sacred text, and because we extract theology, specific doctrines, and commands from it, it is often used technically. Arguments in theology often rely on minor points in the text. When an argument is made based on such minor points, it is extremely important to understand those points correctly.[8]

For those who do not read the Biblical languages, there is a further burden in that you are limited by the choices made by translators. But don't despair! It is possible to work around this difficulty to a significant extent. We will never downplay the benefits of Biblical languages. They are a wonderful tool for personal Bible study. But due to an abundance of English translations, and indeed Spanish, French, and German translations, there are quite a number of very useful tools to allow the person who reads no Greek or Hebrew to study effectively.

There are five areas we want to emphasize in accurately reading a Biblical text. We intend these five areas to be applied to serious study of small portions of scripture. Earlier we discussed overview reading of large portions. Both the purpose and the method for that type of reading is very different from what we're discussing here. The areas are:

1. Use of multiple translations
2. Clarifying key words
3. Examining some options for small words

---

8   To study more deeply about doctrines and certain, we recommend Leslie Newbigin's book *Proper Confidence* (Grand Rapids: Wm B. Eerdman's Publishing Company, 1995, ISBN: 0-8028-0856-5).

4. Outlining
5. Questioning

This entire discussion is designed to help you examine a text of scripture and extract the maximum meaning from that passage. This process will be very different from choosing a topic, and then searching for verses that relate to that topic, or choosing a doctrinal position, and creating a Bible study to support it. Ideally, this kind of detailed study would precede the latter two activities, so that you would be confident that you had chosen your verses correctly.

Reading Out Loud

In ancient times everybody read things out loud. When Philip encounters the Ethiopian eunuch, he hears him reading (Acts 8:30-33). Today we emphasize fast reading and so are generally taught to read silently. But you can get a great deal from reading out loud, either to yourself or to others.

Scriptures such as Psalms cannot be fully experienced unless read aloud. Most prophetic oracles were originally given orally and only later put in written form. You can get more of the feel of a passage and its setting when reading out loud.

In addition, when you read out loud you can't skip over parts of a passage as you can when you read silently. It is a more multisensory approach utilizing both visual and auditory senses.

Praying While Reading

We have suggested an attitude of prayer throughout reading, but one additional approach we have found helpful is to read a passage of scripture and then pray for people and situations as the passage, and the Holy Spirit, may suggest.

This differs from praying the scripture which usually finds promises and then applies them to a particular situation, using the words of scripture in the prayer. Instead, you may find a character in the story who suggests to you someone you know, or perhaps a situation that reminds you to pray.

Multiple Translations

One thing that helps with overview reading is the use of multiple Bible translations. In the previous chapter we suggested the use of three different Bible versions. Reading and comparing these different versions will help you get a clearer view of the text and may also suggestion some questions or new areas for study.

Now, how do you use these versions?

Get your overview, preferably of the whole book, but at least of a few chapters on either side of your passage using your overview Bible. Use your second version, which I'll call your study Bible, to study the details of the passage. Here is where you'll find words to look up in the concordance, dictionary, or Bible dictionary. You'll use that same version for any outlining and phrasing. Wherever you see wordings that make you wonder, or raise questions, compare those wordings to the third version. At some point after you have done most of your study work, you should re-read the passage in all three versions to alert you to any possible translation issues that you might not have noticed.

If you have other Bibles on your shelf, or are working with Bible study software, you may want to look at any difficult passages in a display of all versions. This may help you clarify your understanding.

You will probably find that sometimes there are issues on which you cannot become completely certain. In those cases, you should leave the matter for further study, or if you are sharing with a class or study group, tell people what the options are and why you are uncertain, and don't be dogmatic about it. It doesn't hurt to say that you don't know, or to leave things for further study.

For a chart of some useful Bible versions, see page 22.

Reading in Context

It is important to read a text in context, but frequently "context" is used as an excuse. Someone will suggest that a text has a certain meaning, somebody else says, "You're taking it out of context," and the conversation ends.

Learn to understand just what it is about the context that impacts the meaning.

People usually think of context as a single thing. But each text has a number of different contexts, and different types of literature need to be considered differently. Here are some types of context:

- **Syntactical Context**
  This is simply the linguistic structure of the verse, and how various elements of it fit together. It means you need to get various clauses and phrases attached to the right element of the sentence.
- **Literary Context**
  This is the place where this element fits in the broader structure of the passage you're reading. In part, this involves understanding what type of literature you are reading. You can also consider the rhetorical structure, but that is beyond the scope of this book.
- **Historical Context**
  When in history was this passage written? What were the circumstances? What elements of the history contribute to the nature of the material written.
- **Cultural Context**
  This overlaps with historical context, but goes beyond it. How did the people who wrote and/or heard the piece of literature you are studying understand the world, and written texts? What concepts were available in their world?

- **Canonical Context**
  Where does this passage fit in the overall canon of scripture. For those who are reading the Bible as part of the literature of their faith, this is particularly important. There are reasons why these texts were chosen and put together into the larger book we call the Bible. How does your passage fit into this broader picture?
- **Spiritual or Experiential Context**
  What is the nature of the religious or spiritual experience of the people who wrote and read or heard the passage you are studying?

Question

An excellent technique for digging deeper into a Bible text is to formulate questions about the text, and then look for answers to those questions.

A starting point for this is simply to ask basic fact questions about the text. Many difficult and angry debates about the meaning of a text result from one or more persons not carefully reading what it says. Very frequently, a person is making a very good point, but the text they are quoting doesn't explicitly support that point. Asking fact questions about your text can prevent you from making this error. In your sharing, you can also help defuse such arguments by suggesting that all parties go back and look at the text. That may not make you agree, but it will help clarify what you are discussing.

Consider Genesis 6:5-8. Here are some good example questions:

1. **Who is speaking in this passage?**
   We have a narrator who tells us what God observed (v. 5) and how God responded (v. 6). Then we have the words of God, reported by our narrator, saying God's attitude and God's intention to act ("*I* will wipe ... humanity from the face of the ground"). Then we have

the narrator again to inform us that Noah found grace
(v. 8).

2. **What is God's response?**
God repents or is sorry.

3. **What does God promise to do?**
To destroy human beings and all living things.

4. **Who finds grace?**
Noah.

There are a few more possible questions and some of these are
bound to seem overly simple to you. But it is a good idea to
make sure that you notice *precisely* what the passage says and
what it does not. It's easy to misremember an inference as a
statement when one is not looking directly at the text itself.

In addition, you need to look at questions about the meaning of
the text from different perspectives.

You will frequently find that the first question raised in studying
this passage deals with God's justice, and whether God would
actually kill that many people. Were they all absolutely evil? Was
there no way to save them? Those questions show a personal
perspective – what is God telling me today from this verse? But
you have to first ask what the passage meant originally, and then
follow the track through to a present application.

There are at least three viewpoints on this passage, and Bible
students should be able to think of a fourth pretty quickly. First,
we have Noah himself, to whom God first addresses these
words. Noah is inside the story and things are happening to him.
The second perspective is that of the Israelites, for whom the
story was written. Whether you believe this was written by
Moses himself, or produced later and added to a compilation, it
was still intended to address the people of Israel, presumably
about some situation(s) that they faced. Finally, we must look at
what this story means to us.

If you're wondering, the fourth view that might be helpful would be that of Jesus (Matthew 24:38-39), who used the flood as an illustration of his Second Coming and the last days.

In the first instance, we can ask what Noah's situation might have been when God approached him. If we take the story as it stands, we might expect that Noah felt besieged and hopeless. It is possible that he was threatened by violence. You can ask yourself just what Noah's situation was when God sent the flood. It's fine to speculate on that, and in fact that is much better than to simply make an assumption without thinking about it. I find that most people assume a world that is carrying on quite nicely, but God doesn't like it, and is upset about a little bit of bad behavior, so he gets Noah to build an ark. Then Noah builds it and escapes.

But supposing instead that there was a world on the edge of cataclysmic destruction. We don't know what they were up to, but they could have been about to die in a plague, or they could have been about to wipe themselves out in wars, and take Noah and his family with them. It's not impossible to imagine that the flood, with the ark itself, simply saved one righteous family from a destruction that was going to happen one way or another. I don't necessarily mean that they were going to bring a flood on themselves. They could have merely been about to kill Noah and his family and then wipe each other out in wars over a period of time. Sometimes the application of a limited amount of violence (and the flood was limited, even though those limits were pretty broad) can be used to prevent even greater violence and destruction.

Now keep in mind that we don't know that this second scenario is true either. We present it simply to emphasize that the previous assumption of a world that was prospering though wicked, is also an assumption. The text doesn't specify.

With that thought in mind let's move forward to the time of the Israelites who would be reading this story for the first time. It makes no difference if you think they first read it during the Exodus itself, during the time of the judges, the monarchy, or even after the exile, a similar message can be heard. The crowd can go massively against God, and can get into sin (think "behavior that is destructive of self and of others") beyond the point of no return. God will judge and intervene at some point, but God will also provide a way of escape. Even if there is only one righteous family that needs rescue, God will provide a way of escape. Can you see how that message might have been heard as one of grace under those circumstances?

Consider Abraham's argument with God over Sodom (Genesis 18). He talked God down to 10 righteous people – if there were only 10 righteous people, then God would save Sodom. Do you notice that there are less people than that who are saved in the flood? God's grace doesn't require a certain number.)

To look again from our perspective, what does this tell us? Well, ask how we are similar to the Israelites and how we are different? How much must the message change for this text to apply to your community, your church, your world?

I talked recently to a Marine that just started coming to church for the first time in his life. While serving in Iraq, He was sent a an Special Armed Forces Bible. He started reading it from the beginning but it didn't mean anything to him. He found the Bible difficult to read and irrelevant to his life, but when he got to the story of Noah it clicked. God would be with him and protect him from trouble. From his perspective, he saw the story of Noah as offering great comfort. He felt that God was telling him that he would be with him and protect him despite the danger he was facing.

In reading a Bible story, ask the questions in that order, starting with the people who are inside the story, then looking for those for whom the story was first written, then looking at how your situation is similar to and/or different from the situation of those in the story or its first hearers/readers. You'll be amazed at how often the story becomes directly relevant.[9]

There is much more that can be said about the presentation of the flood story, but these few ideas should get you started. Remember: It's God's story and you're becoming a part of it.

Research

You now need to dig deeper. If you are dealing with questions of fact, you may need to make use of the various resources you collected when you prepared for your study. Each question that you answer may produce new questions. That's why we call this the central loop. You may do this several times.

In addition, you need to work on understanding the structure in more detail.

Clarify Key Words

Often in Bible study we make the assumption that we understand the English wording precisely, when we do not. There are two steps to clarifying key words:

1. Look up English words in a standard dictionary If your version is reasonably modern (and we don't recommend doing serious study from the **King James Version**, **English Revised Version**, or **American Standard Version** because of archaic language), your translators were trying to express the meaning of the text in current English. Make sure you see the options. In serious study, if you are in any doubt about the precise meaning of a word in a verse, look it up, and find any definitions that fit in context. Then as you study further, you can focus in on the precise definition that fits in *your* context.

---

9   When a story doesn't seem relevant, you might also consider how *you* may need to change so *you* can become relevant to *God's* story.

2. Look up Bible place names, personal names, and theological terms in a Bible dictionary. (In the case of theological terms, you can also use a theological dictionary.) Be open to the possibility that you may want to refine your understanding of the word because of its precise meaning in the current context, but start with the hard work other people have done for you.[10]

Examine Options for Small Words

Small English words like *by*, , *of*, and *for*, among many, many others often carry a great deal of freight. For example, the word *of* is often used as part of the translation of the Greek genitive.

In Revelation 19:10, for example, we have the statement, translated literally, "The testimony of Jesus is the spirit of prophecy." You'll find that many versions translate this as "spirit that inspired the prophets" or something similar. Another possibility allowed by the form, though probably not by context, might be "spirit that is prophecy." The little word *of* translates a Greek genitive (the word "prophecy" is in the genitive case) which in Greek indicates a range of relationships between words. So that one little *of* can carry a lot of freight.

Another example is found in Mark 1:4. Here we are told that John came proclaiming "a baptism of repentance for the forgiveness of sins." In this case there can be a number of interpretations. Did the baptism cause the repentance, result from the repentance, symbolize the repentance, complete the repentance, or something else? Does the baptism or the repentance cause the forgiveness, lead to the forgiveness, or display a forgiveness that is already received? All of these issues hang on these little words.

---

10 Some good Bible dictionaries are: *The New International Dictionary of the Bible*, the *New Interpreter's Bible Dictionary*, the *HarperCollins Bible Dictionary*, and the *Anchor Bible Dictionary*.

Think of the various options and compare translations. Normally multiple translations will use different phrasing to represent the different relations between those words, and this can give you an idea of where to go as you study deeper into the verse. Normally, the context will make it quite clear what the precise relationship is, but if you don't realize what options you have, you may settle for forcing a less natural option to work.

Outlining

Outlining seems complicated to many people, but it really is a simple process, partly because there is no absolutely required way to do it. The idea is to pick out the key points in the passage, and relate them to one another. You can use as many layers as you want. Normally, outlines are numbered with some succession of characters and indented indicating the level of each element. A fully detailed outline can end up containing almost all the text of the passage.

Avoid going to that level of detail – it tends to defeat the usual purpose of outlining, which is to make the key points stand out. An outline might look like this:

I. Main point

    1. Sub point
        a. Next level down
        b. Next level down
    2. Another sub point

II. Next main point

    1. etc.

We will provide an example of outlining in parallel with questioning in the exercise for this chapter.

Questioning

By *questioning*, we don't mean doubting the text, though you should not exclude doubts that come up. The idea is to come to God through the medium of the Bible with questions about your life. It's not the questions that hurt!

But as part of your study, you need to ask the obvious questions. What is the main topic (you'll need to know this for outlining as well)? What precisely is the writer telling me about that main topic? Is he talking about people in general, or one specific person? As you study, other questions will come up. You will benefit by having either a study group or by making opportunities to share. Other people will have different questions, and their different perspective may help you get a deeper understanding of the text.

Your fact questions generally deal with what the passage says, and what it meant to the people who first heard it. What elements does it include specifically? Are there things that it does not make any comment on?

Example: Read the story of Elijah on Mt. Carmel (1 Kings 17 & 18).

How many prophets of Baal were there? How long was it between when Elijah called fire from heaven and when the rain came? Asking and answering this kind of question lets you clarify your understanding of what the facts are.

Thought questions start where fact questions finish, and they lead you all the way to application. Is it a good idea to stand up to large numbers of armed opponents the way that Elijah did? Why or why not? What similar situations might I face today?

Here are some more fact questions: Who was Baal? What were the characteristics of the worship of Baal? How did Baal worship compare to the Israelite worship of Yahweh? Some of these questions will require you to go back to the background material and do further research. These questions might lead you to this thought question: How does my worship compare or contrast with the worship of Baal and the worship of Yahweh? You might narrow this down by asking specifically how your prayers (in this case petitions) to God compare to those of the prophets of Baal, and how they compare to the prayer of Elijah. Are there some changes this might suggest for your own prayer life?

You can use outlining at this stage, comparison to other scriptures, to writers in church history, or to current experience. Ask: What similar experience are we having today? Can this help me understand the passage? For example, if you have had a dream or vision will that help you understand Ezekiel's vision in Ezekiel 1? Ask your friends about experiences they have had. (See *Chapter 16:Visions and Dreams.*).

Some historical writers you might consult include John Chrysostom, Jerome, Aquinas, Augustine, Martin Luther, John Wesley, John Calvin, Charles Spurgeon, Karl Barth, and many, many others.

Don't be afraid to repeat this process a number of times. Sometimes after I have meditated on the details for awhile, I will read the passage through quickly again, or even read it two or three times more. Once I have looked at more details, different things start to stand out.

Compare

The next element of the central loop is "compare."

This involves a very common principle, that scripture is its own best interpreter. It's also called "comparing scripture with scripture." But this process of comparison can be dangerous. It's very easy to turn comparing scripture with scripture into combining random phrases from one scripture with random phrases from another, and when that happens the result can be absolutely anything.

So how do you compare?

Remember that each passage you study is part of an act of communication. It was given under its own circumstances at a particular time and place. In order to sensibly compare passages, you have to understand both passages and how they are related.

Here are some of the basics:

1. Whenever you compare two scriptures, be sure you have carefully studied both passages.
2. Look for the relationship.
    a. Is one copying or quoting the other?
    b. Is one alluding to the other?
    c. Are they talking about the same subject?
    d. Is one the fulfillment of something predicted in the other?
    e. Do they use common symbolism, metaphors, or other languages?
3. Avoid the assumption that a word defined one way in one passage necessarily means the same thing in another. Words have a range of meaning, and can have different precise definitions in different passages. Hebrews 11:1 says that faith is "the substance of things that are not seen," and in Mark 5:34 Jesus tells the woman with the issue of blood that her faith has saved/healed her. The range of meaning of "faith" (Greek *pistis*) covers both instances, but we're not looking at precisely the same point.
4. Be sure you're aware of the focus and the key point(s) of each passage. You can't compare two passages correctly unless you understand each one in its own context.
5. Be sure you're aware of who's speaking. For example, people frequently quote from the speeches of Job's friends as support for particular theological positions, but God doesn't appear to be very impressed (see Job 38:1).
6. Don't let comparing scripture with scripture keep you from hearing what each author is saying. It's easy, for example, to explain away James by quoting Paul, but

perhaps it would be good to fully hear what James has to say before combining the two.

7. Don't assume that all Bible cross-references are valid. Just because someone printed it in a Bible note doesn't make it true. Check for yourself.

Many of these points could do with considerably more discussion, but this is a good start.

Conclusion

Remember that the precise approach to a passage will be determined by the type of literature that it is. You will need to adapt your method to the material you are studying.

Exercise

Use the following outline and questions from Colossians as an example, then outline Philippians 1:1-14 and write your own questions. You can compare and contrast the openings of these two epistles.

Colossians 1:1-14 - Outlining and Questioning

The following illustrates the outlining and questioning process.

Point Outline

1. Greeting (1-2)
2. Thanks for what God has done (3-8)
3. Prayer for God's continued activity (9-14)

The points in this outline align with the paragraph breaks in most Bibles. This point outline doesn't give us much information. It simply tells us in general what Paul is trying to do in these verses. Let's try a little more detailed of an outline.

Detailed Outline

1. Greeting (1-2)
   (a) Paul and Timothy writing together
2. Address to the saints and faithful ones in Colossae
3. Standard wish for grace and peace
4. Thanks for what God has done (3-8)
   (a) Paul and Timothy pray constantly
5. Gospel is bearing fruit in Colossae as it is elsewhere
6. Epaphras taught them
   (a) He is a fellow-laborer of Paul and Timothy
7. He is a faithful servant
8. Prayer for God's continued activity (9-14)
   (a) Prayer continues that they would grow
9. Same faith is bearing fruit there as in all the world
10. They work according to God's power
11. Jesus is their redeemer

There are any number of things you could change in that outline. Don't use it as is, but as an exercise, criticize it and make it work for you.

Questions

♦ Why does Paul specify that he is an apostle "by the will of God?" Aren't all apostles appointed by the will of God?
   Look at some of the openings to Paul's other letters to give you a hint.
♦ What is it Paul is thanking God for?
♦ What defines the "genuine word of the good news?"
♦ What are Paul's major aims or desires for the church in Colossae?
♦ Is both their faith and their love the result of the hope laid up for them in heaven?
♦ Why is God the Father, rather than Jesus specified as the one who redeemed us from the authority of darkness?

You will undoubtedly think of many more questions.

Now try to outline Philippians 1:1-14 and write a series of study questions. If you have time, compare and contrast the openings of these two epistles.

8

Share your Thoughts

Sharing is critical both for living as a witness and for being accountable

In the participatory Bible study method, the final stage is sharing. It is last on the list because you have to dig into your Bible study in order to have something to share, but *not* because it is the least important.

Often when we emphasize sharing in Bible study, the response is blank stares. Surely sharing is something you do after you have studied, not a part of your study. But sharing is a learning experience for you, not simply a time when you can inform others of what you have learned.

The biggest threat to learning about the Bible (or any other subject) is the assumption that you already know what the Bible is saying. One of the best ways to counter that threat is by engaging in dialogue with others. They will help you see the text from a different and often more informed perspective.

Ask yourself how this has applied in your experience. Get to know the person you are sharing with. Share your experience and then the text. Always work from your own personal experience with God.

Store up the experiences your friends share with you to use in studying further scripture.

Some basic ideas:

- Sharing forces you to think more clearly about what you study, because you have to learn how to communicate it with someone else who may have a different perspective.

- Sharing lets you hear the perspective of someone else so you can expand your own understanding.

- Sharing can allow you to get information from someone else that you hadn't known or considered.

- Sharing provides accountability so you don't go too far with personal, eccentric interpretations.

Here are the guidelines for sharing that are included in each participatory study guide:

GUIDELINES FOR SHARING

1. **Sharing does not mean that you find something you can tell someone else.** You may find something to tell someone, but you may also find something you would like to learn from someone else.
2. **Think about what you can learn.** What is it that you could gain by listening to what someone else says?
3. **Think about what the other person needs and wants to hear, not about what you need to say.** You may have a very helpful thought, but you may share it with someone who is dealing with completely different problems and cannot relate to what you share.
4. **Even when you share something by speaking to someone, be prepared to listen to their response.** The time for listening is always now.
5. **Don't be discouraged when people don't get as excited as you are about your discovery.** They may not be at a place in their lives where they can use it, or they may have discovered it years ago just when they needed it, and it's old now.
6. **Listen more than you talk.**

Exercise

1. Find out what study opportunities are available in your church or other community. Include:

    ◆   Teachers, pastors, and other persons with specific expertise that might be helpful in your study.

    ◆   People with practical experience of the church and of life.

    ◆   Study groups.

    ◆   Sunday School classes

    How can these people or groups enhance your Bible study?

2. Choose a passage for Bible study, preferably one that has troubled you in the past. Try to write five questions about that passage that you can ask someone else. Who will you ask?

3. Find a particular note of encouragement in your Bible study during this coming week. Try to find someone who has a particular need for that particular encouraging note. Remember, you will have to observe and listen in order to find the right person with whom to share.

4. Make a special point in your prayers to ask God's guidance in making your personal Bible study more of a community activity.

5. Write down what you learned from you study of the Bible in a journal like it was a devotion. Consider sharing it with a small group or use e-mail, Facebook, Twitter, or other social media to share it with friends.

6. Take a moment to pray about what core message God is giving you during your Bible study. Try to figure out

why you need to hear that message.   Make a list of other people who are in a similar circumstance as you who may also need to hear the same word. Pray for the people on the list and see if it would be appropriate or possible to share what you learned in study with them.

LIVING

... and is useful for teaching, for reproof, for correction, and for
training in righteousness, so that everyone who belongs to God may
be proficient, equipped for every good work.
    –   *2 Timothy 3:16-17 (NRSV)*

9

Types of Literature

*What types of literature can you find in the Bible and
what difference does this make?*

Note: This chapter is one of those rare cases where it
may be profitable to complete the exercises first and then
read the chapter. If you are doing this study in a group,
consider doing the exercises before anyone has looked at
the discussion. (Go to page 61.)

Now that we have examined the main points of the method, we
are going to use the remainder of this book to look at the
various types of literature in the Bible and how we study them.

Many people are used to thinking of the Bible as a book, and
thinking of one approach to Bible study. The Bible as a whole is
to be studied in a particular way that is different from the way
we study other books.

But the Bible was not always a single book. It is a collection of
books, and some of those books are themselves collections.

For example, the book of Proverbs was first a general collection
of sayings, then those sayings were collected into various groups,
and finally those groups were put together into what we now call
the book of Proverbs.

How do we know this? The book of Proverbs itself tells us. In
chapter one, verse one, we are told that these are sayings of
Solomon. This formula is repeated elsewhere in the book. In
Proverbs 25:1 we are told that these are proverbs of Solomon

and that King Hezekiah's men copied them. In chapter 30, we have the words of Agur.

So not only do we have one book within the book we call the Bible, and one that is quite unique, we also have parts within that book that are not identical. Proverbs 8:22-31 is a song about wisdom and its place in creation. This is part of a larger complex of connected texts over the first several chapters of the book. Later, however, we will have lists of largely unconnected sayings.

The way we read these lists of sayings is not the same as the way we read the longer selections in the early chapters. For example, we might tell someone a verse is taken out of context, when they build something on a single verse without considering what comes before and after. But look at this passage:

> 14   Where there is no guidance, a nation falls,
> but in an abundance of counselors there is safety.
> 15   To guarantee loans for a stranger brings trouble,
> but there is safety in refusing to do so.
> 16   A gracious woman gets honor,
> but she who hates virtue is covered with shame.
> The timid become destitute,
> but the aggressive gain riches. – *Proverbs 11:14-16 (NRSV)*

If you are interpreting verse 15, in what way do the verses that come before and after help you? They do help you decide what kind of literature you're reading, but they don't tell you much about what particular saying in the list means.

There are many types of literature in the Bible, and it is helpful, if not essential to understand what each type is about and to tailor our approach to studying these passages to the particular type of literature.

We don't read a cookbook in the same way as we read a newspaper, and we don't need to read Revelation in the same way as we read Kings either.

Here is a list of the type of literature we will discuss along with some examples:

Type	Examples
Poem	Song of Songs, Psalm 78, 104, 119
Song/Hymn	Song of Miriam (Exodus 15:1-18), Song of Deborah (Judges 5), Psalm 19, 27
Story	Ruth, Esther, many shorter passages
History	1 & 2 Samuel, 1 & 2 Kings, 1 & 2 Chronicles, Nehemiah, Ezra
Parable	Luke 16
Allegory	Ezekiel 16
Doctrinal Teaching	Matthew 5-7
Wisdom Literature	Proverbs, (this may overlap with Poems)
Prophetic Oracle	Isaiah 14:1-23
Vision Report	Ezekiel 1,Daniel 7, 8
Prayer	Psalm 12, Daniel 9
Letter	Romans, 1 & 2 Corinthians, Galatians

There is a key additional ingredient to each type of literature in the Bible. We must never forget that it's God's inspiration. There are many ways in which Bible study is similar to study of other literature, but it is also always more than the study of other literature. As we read texts written by God's servants, we also listen for God's voice.

Exercise

1. Make a list of various types of literature. Try to think as broadly as you can. Some examples include newspaper stories, poetry, weather reports, and so forth. There is a chart provided for you on page (62) so you can make your list. This exercise can be done as a group, but it will help if each member of the group brings some ideas. Think about what kind of information you expect to get from it, and how much time and thought you will put into getting that information.

2. Make a list of types of literature that we find in the Bible. How many of these types of literature are similar to those you found in Exercise 1? Try to do this before you have read the chapter, then see how many more you can think of after you complete your reading. Space is provided on page 63.

Exercise Chart #1: What do you expect of various types of literature you read? The first is an example.

Type of Literature	Kind(s) of Information	Hard to Understand?
Cookbook	Recipes	No

Exercise Chart #2: What types of literature do you find in the Bible? How do they relate to those you read in your daily life? (The first line is an example.)

Type of Literature	Kind(s) of Information	Hard to Understand?
Poetry	*Characteristics of God*	*No (your answer may differ!)*

10

Stories

Studying Bible stories and learning to apply them in your own life

Various types of stories in the Bible require a different approach to interpretation than do more informational items such as **epistles**, visions, wisdom literature, or prophetic books. Often stories are neglected in favor of material that gets more directly to the point. Many would rather interpret the Sermon on the Mount than a story of Jesus healing someone. Nonetheless, a large portion of the Bible consists of stories, and often those elements that are not themselves stories suggest a background story (1 Corinthians, for example, clearly responds to some specific events and incidents and interpreters find it helpful to try to figure out what these were).

Stories are important because it is through stories that we understand our lives. The Gospel is itself a story about the way that God sees and saves the world. Any preacher knows the power of a story. People rarely remember quotes for even main point a week later, but some people will remember a story forever.

Remembering the Basics

The participatory study method looks at certain key questions in relation to each scripture passage. While we will list some more detailed and specific elements, let's remember the more general key elements:

- ◆ What is the experience behind this passage?

- How might the experience reflected in this passage relate to my own experience?
- What principle(s) lies behind the specific statements?
- How might the principles relate to my life?

Now let's look at how we find these elements in a story.

Let's distinguish various types of stories. In the Bible we find some simple, short stories, some of which stand alone, but others are part of a longer series, or of a history. For example, the story of Elijah on Mt. Carmel is a single short story (we studied it earlier), but it is also part of a series of stories that feature Elijah and his conflict with the Israelite monarchy, especially Ahab, over the worship of Baal. It combines into the longer series of Elijah-Elisha narratives, and these form a part of the history of the northern Kingdom of Israel that is told in 1 Kings 12 through 2 Kings 17, intertwined with stories of Judah.

Such stories can be either true or fictional, or sometimes fictionalized. By "fictionalized" we mean that a true story has been adjusted in details to help make the point that the narrator desired. In general, it will matter very little whether a story is true, fictionalized, or pure fiction when we interpret it. Only when we're dealing with a broader history does the historical accuracy become important to our understanding. This is not to suggest that any specific story is fictional or fictionalized, but it would be most common for parables to have a fictional element.

Besides short stories, we will also find parables, very often told by Jesus, allegory (i.e. Ezekiel 16), and history. We will discuss how to interpret parables, allegory, and history separately, but for now it is important to distinguish the type of narratives. A parable may be a true story, or simply be made up on the spot, but it is told generally to make one key point. Even if it is a true story, the person who tells it or writes it is not intending us to get something out of every detail. In addition, the point of telling the story is not so that we will know what happened, but rather so that we will learn from it. The story may not tell us what truly happened but it may convey a deep truth about God or the world. It is very important to keep this distinction in mind.

In more general stories, the writer or story teller may be illuminating characters, helping us to understand certain historical circumstances, or providing us with historical details to fill out a more general history. This kind of story is the most subject to our own interpretations, and also is often the most rewarding. We may find much value in the story beyond what the original writer intended by telling it.

Reading the Story

A key element in interpreting stories is imagination. Put aside the search for details. You don't need to make every element of the story teach a profound lesson. It may simply provide some small element of the personality of one of the characters. On the other hand, putting your imagination to work in filling in details, providing a background, and coming to understand how the characters may have felt can be very helpful. St. Ignatius of Loyola developed a reading technique that utilized imagination. He taught that if we imagined with our senses what the story looks like, smelt like, and felt like we might be able to really get into the text.

In a story, you may be hearing directly the experience of the writer and often of the people about whom he is writing. In a doctrinal statement, something is stated about God that results from our experience of God as God acts in our lives. In a story, we can see directly this divine action and how it was experienced by the characters.

Consider the following statement about God: *God rewards those who are faithful to him even when things look bad.*

In the story of Elijah on Mt. Carmel (1 Kings 17 & 18), we have the expression of just such an experience, as Elijah stands for what he believes, even when things look very difficult. The story of Elijah is part of the "raw material" from which the doctrinal statement is made. The simple fact is nice, but the experience sticks in our minds and helps build our faith even more.

(One could suggest a study here of those who don't appear to be rewarded. But then we might consider Stephen, who saw heaven opened and knew of the coming heavenly reward when he was standing and being stoned for what he believed.)

So absorb the narrative as you read it, and let your imagination roam freely in trying to see or feel the parts of the story that aren't stated. Always be aware of what is stated and what you are imagining, but let the story grow for you. Once you have a picture, ask the following question about each character:

Is he or she advancing God's kingdom?

The answer to this question may help you to decide whether a character should be imitated, or whether they might have provided a bad example.

For each action, ask: Is this action something that would advance the kingdom or not?

In the story of Elijah on Mt. Carmel, for example, only Elijah advances God's kingdom. Ahab vacillates, as does the crowd. The priests of Baal are working against God.

Once you have done this, put yourself in the place of one or more of the characters, especially one with whom you have little sympathy. If you are fearless in sharing your faith, perhaps you should put yourself in Ahab's position. Why might Ahab find it hard to make a clear decision? Try to understand the way Ahab thought. Are there admirable qualities about Ahab? What are they? What seems to keep getting in his way as he tries to be a memorable king of Israel?

Throughout all of this, make sure not to look down on the characters. Frequently when Christians study the Bible, we take our 21st century understanding of the world, and the two or three thousand years of history that we have experienced since, and we criticize all the Bible characters for behaving the way they did. But if we were presented with the same set of circumstances and the same knowledge, would we have done better? Make a serious effort to understand just what Ahab knew, and not to put your own knowledge into the picture. This doesn't mean you have to agree with him; just try to understand his attitude.

It is very rare that people set out to be evil or destructive. Usually some good motivations combine with some bad ones and are then followed by some bad choices in how to carry out those not-quite-perfect intentions. If you understand this, you might be able to learn more from the story than if you approach it as someone superior to the characters, who would surely never have made their mistakes.

As an advanced exercise, try to retell the story in the first person as one of the characters present. As an example, let's tell the story of Elijah on Mt. Carmel from Ahab's perspective.

Example: Ahab's Viewpoint

It wasn't a very good day. We were so short on water, and we couldn't find Elijah, the man who had predicted this very famine. I wanted to find him, talk to him, and get him to understand our need. Then he could pray and get Yahweh to call this thing off. I had enough problems with the Syrians raiding from time to time.

All these attacks on Baal worship didn't sit very well with my wife either. Jezebel had grown up as a worshiper of Baal, and she didn't like it very much when I paid attention to the Yahweh party, especially those pesky prophets. But even more than domestic tranquility in the palace, the prophets were risking my alliance with Tyre and Sidon, which were economically so important.

Then along comes Obadiah to tell me that Elijah is back. It's no wonder I called him "Troubler of Israel!" Who else had caused us nearly this much trouble? But even more he couldn't just keep the thing quiet. A sacrifice or so to Yahweh, that I could handle, but public repudiation of Baal? It just wasn't possible! The man may be incredibly spiritual, but he really doesn't comprehend how things work here on solid ground!

But what can you do? It seemed the only chance we had of surviving the drought was to get it called off, and Elijah wanted to do the whole thing publicly. Why? It was a disaster! Either he'd win, in which case Queen Jezebel would be in a sulk for months, and she knew how to sulk effectively, or he would lose, and I'd be left even weaker before the pro-Baal, pro-Tyre element in Israel. Losing was most likely. With friends like Elijah, we'd be a simple **client state** in no time.

Throughout his demonstration on the mountain he just kept making it worse! Of course you couldn't expect rain to come that quickly, much less fire from heaven. No, he had to keep things going. Then he carried out that spectacular miracle. It had to be a trick, but I don't see how he could have done it! Still, it had to be a trick!

But the rain that followed after – no, that couldn't have been a trick. Maybe it was just delayed rain because of the prayers of the Baal prophets. It was delayed enough.

Yes, Elijah won. But what about me? It seems that my kingdom is worse off than it was before. I think I'll just look the other way while Jezebel gets her revenge for the dead prophets.

As a further exercise, take the perspective of a character in the story and try to evaluate the actions of another. For example, we see Elijah as decisive, right, in tune with God, courageous, and powerful. How does Ahab see him? How does the crowd see him, and how does their perspective change?

Application

To complete any of these exercises, look at your own life and ask if you have harbored any of the attitudes or taken any of the actions that you have identified as not advancing God's kingdom. Many of us have probably compromised as Ahab was trying to do. We can argue that we didn't compromise over anything as important. But do you suppose that Ahab's first compromise in life was in allowing the religion of Baal to supplant the worship of Yahweh in his kingdom?

Any story interpretation should include looking at the things we should take as an example and distinguishing them from those we definitely should not imitate. Many stories in the Bible don't comment on the actions of various characters. Silence does not mean that their actions have been approved by God.

Now look through your own life. Have you had any experiences that are similar to this one? Have you had any experiences that may not have been similar, but yet required you to make the same type of decisions? How did your decisions compare to those of the characters in the story?

Extend your search for parallels to those of your family, friends and community. How do the decisions of the various people compare?

Sharing

Ask others about their experiences. When you do this, be sure to show your openness by sharing your own experiences first. Then listen non-judgmentally to their stories. You want to learn from them, and let them learn from yours. That won't happen if you set yourself up as a superior example. Don't judge! Do Share!

Looking Wider

This method is most applicable to smaller, self-contained stories. But after you have studied an individual story in this way, you can continue by studying it in connection with its series. Elijah first appears in 1 Kings 17 and stories continue through 2 Kings 2. The Elijah series leads into the Elisha series.

Exercise

Select a well-known story from the Bible and try telling it from the perspective of one of the characters. For example, you might try telling the story of the prodigal son from the perspective of the prodigal or of his brother.

Here are some stories to try:

1. The Prodigal Son (Luke 15:11-32)

2. Elijah on Mt. Carmel (1 Kings 17 & 18)

3. The Fall (Genesis 3)

11

History

Understanding the history of God's action in the world as told in the Bible story and in the many many Bible books that contain history.

It is easy to think that interpreting history is simply a matter of interpreting a series of stories. If you understand the message of the individual stories, you pretty much have the history, but that is far from the truth. Most historical passages in the Bible have a much broader meaning. History is similar to story in that it tells a broader story like a biography of a person or history of a group.

Historical Accuracy

For the most part one can understand the intention of a story, why it is told, and what lessons one can learn from it, without deciding whether it is true, true-to-life, or fictitious. Fiction can teach a lesson just as well as a true story. But when we are dealing with the telling of history, there is a big difference. When we study history in the Bible, most commonly the writers are trying to tell us something about the way God has acted and will act in the world. More than the individual incidents, the focus is on God's broader plan.

In a document that tells about historical events there can be many focuses and viewpoints. In reading modern history we usually look for a central theme, chronological data, and fairly precise geographical references, this is rarely the intention with the Biblical writers. The gospels, for example, often tell us the stories and various sayings of Jesus in different orders. Is this because they didn't know the historical order or were being careless? Actually, each gospel writer had certain reasons for his approach to telling the story of Jesus. Generally these writings want to tell us who Jesus was, and his impact, and these themes are more important to them than the **chronology**.

In the major histories of Samuel-Kings and Chronicles-Ezra-Nehemiah, the theme of how God worked through Israel is central. There is more chronology in these books than in the gospels, but nonetheless the purpose is not chronology. In the broadest sense these books tell us what God expected of Israel, and how Israel needed to behave in order to receive God's blessing and avoid judgment. This will often explain why details are left out of the history that we would like to know in modern times.

Questions

When you study history, rather than just story, look for applications that are broader: Your family, church, community, or your country. Ask:

- How is the group (family, community, nation) discussed in this passage similar to my own group? Look for duties, laws, relation to God and his divine purpose, and possibilities.
- How is the group different?
- Where does history fit in God's overall plan?
  We understand the Bible to describe an overall plan of God for the world. (If you do not agree, you might ask why the author of the history felt it would fit in that particular time and place.)
- For each character, ask the same questions as you would in a story. Try to look at the history from their point of view. It is easy to blame Saul for his suspicion of David, or David for his lax and unrealistic attitude with his sons.

But it is worthwhile to ask how each of us would act under the same circumstances.

Background

Background information becomes even more important. No history can reflect all aspects of the story, and the Bible stories are really very short for the period of time they cover. There are historical materials from many of the surrounding cultures that we can use to understand the world in which the Israelite people were living. You can be sure that the Assyrians and the Phoenicians felt substantially different about themselves than the Israelites did!

Exercise

1. Compare and contrast the birth and childhood stories of Jesus found in Matthew 1-2 and Luke 1-2. How do the various elements present the theological message that each gospel writer wants to present? You may need to read an introduction to each book to get an overview of the themes of Matthew and Luke.

2. Read Judges 1. This is a summary chapter regarding the period of Israel's history between their entry into the land of Canaan in Joshua and the time of the kings, which begins in 1 Samuel. What are the key messages that the narrator of this history wants to get across?

3. Read an introduction to the book of Joshua, or simply read the entire book quickly. How does the description of the conquest in Joshua differ from that in Judges? What message might each book be trying to convey?

4. Read the story of Philip in Acts 8. This can be treated either as a story or as a part of the history of the early church. Look at Acts 7 and Acts 9. What role does chapter 8 play in the overall history?

12

Parable and Allegory

Looking at the metaphorical and symbolic language in the Bible

There are very few allegorical passages in the Bible, even though people commonly refer to many passages as allegory. **Allegory** is a form of literature in which elements of the narrative represent something other than what they appear on the surface. Characters often embody specific moral or ethical elements. The key to allegory is that most of the elements of the story represent something.

In a parable, on the other hand, there is normally one central point, and many of the characters and elements of the story are simply props to help carry that one theme to conclusion. Whereas in an allegory, almost every element is made to carry some weight. A parable might be defined as a short story or word picture that illus-trates a single point of spiritual truth. There are numerous parables in the Bible.

Identifying Allegory and Parables

There is no firm dividing line between a parable and an allegory. The key to interpreting either one is to determine just what is part of the background of the story and what is intended to carry particular meaning.

To illustrate, consider Luke 15:8-10, the Parable of the Lost Coin. There is a single theme, God seeking the lost which is illustrated through an ordinary experience, the loss of a coin. This is a basic parable. The following story, that of the prodigal son, is still considered a parable, but it adds a few more elements, and is closer to an allegory. For a true allegory, we can look at Ezekiel 16:1-58. Here Israel and Judah are represented by sisters who are rescued by the Lord as he seeks them, but who rebel despite the good things that have been done for them. There is an application in verses 59-63. In this allegory each element--the sisters, their lovers, their clothing, and their various actions are all representative of something. Ezekiel 16 is not precisely like a basic (or prototypical) allegory in that most of the elements represent real, historical persons or places.

The parable of the trees in Judges 9:7-15, is less a parable than an allegory. Here the various types of trees represent various types of people who might live in a country and be invited to be king. Nonetheless there is a single lesson at the end.

Another good example of a basic parable is the parable of the mustard seed (Matthew 13:31-32). Here Jesus uses a small seed producing a large plant as the illustration of the small and unpretentious beginnings of kingdom work among people, which produce great results. There is a single point. It is a simple word picture. It makes the point clearly. In the case of a parable like this one, do not get distracted by issues such as the actual size of a mustard seed, the actual size of the resulting plant, how long the plant takes to grow, or who planted the seed. None of those have anything to do with the main point.

It is somewhat more difficult to deal with the parable of the sower (Matthew 13:1-9). Here Jesus tells a slightly more extended story, and uses more individual elements as meaningful. But there is still a central point: The kingdom is planted far and wide, but it does not bear fruit everywhere. In the interpretation provided in verses 18-23, we have meanings attached to many elements of the parable. This is similar to the way one understands an allegory. Note that many scholars believe that we are hearing the voice of the early church in the explanation, as they made use of the teaching of Jesus in their day to day lives. It's OK to try to milk this parable for everything you can get from it before looking at the interpretation. There was a reason that Jesus spoke in parables, rather than simply giving the interpretation in the first place.

Parables make you think, and help you make the truth expressed more a part of yourself than a simple statement would. They are also more likely to be remembered. Thus the parables themselves act much like the seed that is described in this parable. Each person is free to get as little or as much from the parable as he or she desires.

Allegory in Other Types of Literature

Much of what we interpret allegorically in the Bible actually occurs in other types of literature. Paul uses the story of Hagar and Sarah (Galatians 4:24) as an allegory of the two covenants. When a story is interpreted allegorically, one need not use all of the elements of the story in the allegorical interpretation. In Galatians, Paul uses the two women, Sarah and Hagar, and the fact that one was free and one was a slave, along with the blessing on Isaac's seed to represent the nature and future of two covenants. He doesn't refer to many other elements of the story, such as Abraham's role, God's protection of Hagar and his promise concerning Ishmael, or Sarah's role in throwing Ishmael and Hagar out of the house.

The book of Hebrews uses the future rest for Israel, which originally dealt with their settling in the promised land, as a sort of allegory for the Christian walk and the future blessing of rest for God's people in the heavenly kingdom. (This material starts at Hebrews 3:7, but continues through the rest of the argument of that book.) In this way, the exodus from Egypt, the troubles of the wilderness wandering, and the difficulties of the conquest can become an illustration of the Christian life, either of a group or of an individual.

This interpretation has become an important part of modern Christian thinking and experience, especially in the charismatic community. Christians are admonished to "take the land" which is a reference to the exodus, and to its allegorical interpretation as a description of the Christian life, both individually and as a community.

Some Dangers in Allegorical Interpretation

Once I was teaching a group of people, working on a Bible overview, and I used this allegorical interpretation of the exodus and the conquest. One woman in my class became more and more upset as I continued to work through the allegory. When it was time for questions, she asked, "But still those were real people suffering and dying, weren't they?"

I intended to eventually discuss the history, but I hadn't gotten there at that point. She brought up one of the dangers of allegorical interpretation, especially of stories or histories: It is very easy to get attached to the allegory, and lose all of the meaning of the original story. This does not mean that an allegorical interpretation is bad, especially when that interpretation draws on the principles that lie behind the history.

An allegory may come from the author (such as Ezekiel 16), or be part of the reader's interaction with the story. It is important to know the difference. If we believe that the Bible is inspired, we should try to find out what it says, not what we can make it say. Allegorical interpretation can be a way of imposing our theology and philosophy on the text of the Bible, rather than allowing the scriptures to lead us.

Sometimes allegory is used to get around the meaning of a passage. It is often used very loosely, as when anything that simply won't fit is called allegorical. "Don't take that too literally!" is a frequent comment, which often means, "Ignore that!" Genesis 1-3 are often dismissed as either allegory (which they are not) or as mythology. They do share some characteristics with the form of literature we know as mythology, especially in chapters two and three. But Genesis 1:1-2:4 share almost none of characteristics of mythology, and certainly do not look like intended allegory.

Does this mean that they must be taken literally? Actually there are many alternatives other than "allegorical" and "literal." We believe Genesis 1 is liturgy, for example, intended for use in celebrating the creation in worship. It thus does not need to be narrative history, nor does it need to provide a chronology, but it nonetheless describes God's involvement in creation.

Dangers of allegorical interpretation:

+ Forgetting the intended meaning
+ Using the allegory as *the* interpretation
  Sometimes an allegory can be helpful, but unless you are sure that the author intended to write allegorically, don't use it to prove a point.
+ Wild flights of fancy
  Allegorical interpretation is already just a bit loose, provided that the allegory is not intended by the author, and unless one is careful, one can simply create one's own world of meaning completely detached from the text.
+ Calling something allegory in order to avoid what it says (See comments on Genesis above)

Don't Be Afraid of Allegory

Despite these cautions, understanding allegory, and even using allegorical interpretations of portions of the Bible can be an extremely rewarding type of study. Allegory has a rich history in Christianity, including much early Christian interpretation of the Old Testament. Don't be afraid of allegory; use it wisely!

Exercise

Write your own parable on the importance of reading the Bible.
This story could be allegorical where each character is symbolic
of something or it could revolve around a simple theme.

13

Poetry

Understanding Biblical poetry and how it differs from modern English poetry

Much of the Bible, especially the Hebrew Bible or Old Testament, is written in poetic form. There are many things that cannot be explained in stories or in history. If you were 'in love' with someone you could write them a six point paper of their qualities but a love poem would be more appropriate.

Poetry helps to describe things that are indescribable. There is a scene in the Carl Sagan movie *'Contact'* where the main character finally meets with the Extra-terrestrial beings in a scene that resembles meeting God in heaven. She then comments that they should not have sent a scientist on this mission of exploration "they should have sent a poet." The God that the Bible speaks of is beyond our words. Poetry is a useful tool to help us get a slightly better picture of who this God is.

It is important to understand some characteristics of poetry in general, and specifically about Hebrew poetry in particular, in order to understand these passages properly. In many cases, the poetic passages will also fall under one of the other categories of literature in the Bible, such as prayers, hymns or prophetic oracles. In these cases, you will find that understanding the poetic form will supplement other methods of study.

Basics of Interpreting Poetry

There are some basic characteristics of poetry . These include:

1. In interpreting poetry you may find examples in which the poetry reflects accurately what was said, but is not intended as truth in terms of its content. As an example, think of the speeches of Job's friends. They are accurate, we would assume, but are the sentiments they express true?[11] When God comes on the scene, he says they are not (Job 38:1-2), and indeed condemns the speakers. Thus it is a bad idea to use their words as the basis for theology. One should be very careful in applying this principle; it would be easy to say, "That passage doesn't apply to me. It's just there illustrating someone's view." But it does apply in some cases. I would suggest Psalm 137 as an example, particularly verses 8 & 9, which could easily be a statement of how the Israelites felt, and thus recorded for us, but not a statement of how a Christian *should* feel.

2. Again, in poetry, an expression can be abbreviated, and thus less clear than we would expect a prose statement to be. In this case, you're already applying the right principle, which is to find what God says elsewhere more clearly, and shape your understanding of the poetic passage to that. As a key principle we believe that all scripture interpretation should "hang your interpretation on the two commandments." Jesus says that all the law and the prophets should hang on these two (Matthew 22:40), so if you can't hang them there, you may be off track. (Note that sometimes it's a misunderstanding of what love is, not a misunderstanding of some particular passage that is the problem.)

---

11 'Accuracy' in dialog may reflect either what a character actually said, or a fictional character with comments appropriate to his or her role in the story. It does not necessarily mean "precisely what a particular person said at the time."

3. Poetry frequently uses more metaphorical or symbolic language than other forms of literature.

4. Poetry frequently uses more obscure words in order to fill the forms. You need to be cautious about understanding the word precisely as it is used in its context. In the case of Biblical poetry, you will find more differences between translations of poetry because some of the vocabulary is obscure. Hebrew poetry uses many synonyms (see the discussion of parallelism below) and this often results in use of less common vocabulary. In many cases, poetry uses words that occur only once in the Bible or even in all Hebrew literature that we have available. This can result in disagreements. (See the section Reading the Text Precisely, page 34).

Hebrew Poetry

While it seems likely that Hebrew poetry did use certain types of meter, there is so much controversy about precisely how this works that it remains a subject for the experts to argue about, and not a practical tool for the Bible student. Fortunately, the main characteristic of Hebrew poetry is 'thought parallelism', in which the relationships of the meaning of elements of the lines of poetry carry a substantial part of the meaning of the whole poem.

There are three types of parallelism that are most common, and also of most practical use to the Bible student:

1. **Synonymous**
   Elements of the poetic lines are either synonymous or have overlapping semantic ranges in which the second line completes the meaning of the first.

2. **Antithetical**
   Elements of the poetic lines are opposite to one another.

3. **Synthetic**
   Elements of the poetic line build on one another, but are

not related as synonymous or antithetical, for example, the first line states an event, and the second states a conclusion. Since these groups of poetic lines can be interpreted much like prose, I will concentrate here on the first two.

Note that the line between these may be a bit blurred, and you will see some combinations of more than one style, and some that will be hard to classify.

Elements may be dropped from any line of poetry, and carried over from a previous line. We gave an example of this in chapter so we're skipping that example here.

Synonymous Parallelism

| From | your rebuke | they fled; |
| From voice | your thunderous | they rushed away. |

Psalm 104:7 (rearranged slightly to show the elements)

In interpreting synonymous parallelism, try thinking of the meaning of the verse as a single statement. Don't try to make a new thought out of the second (or third) line of poetry. This is especially important in Proverbs, where there can be a temptation to make theology out of half a Proverb, and then build a new thought out of the second half. The two or three lines of synonymous parallelism act together to express a single thought more completely.

Antithetical Parallelism

| The legacy | of the righteous | is blessing; |
| But the name (or reputation) | of the wicked | will rot. |

Proverbs 10:7

Here the thought of the first line is expanded by expressing its opposite in the next line. In interpreting the passage, again remember that we are not looking at two different thoughts. The single thought is the difference between the legacy (or remembrance) of a righteous person and a wicked person. The antithetical parallelism helps create a contrast between the results of the life of each one.

Note: An interesting exercise in interpreting poetry, and more broadly in understanding Biblical inspiration, is to compare the thought of this short proverb, and the book of Ecclesiastes. For example, look at the fatalism in Ecclesiastes 2:12-17. What is the point of each? How are they expressed? Compare and contrast them. Look back to the principles expressed at the beginning of this essay for some suggestions on finding the truth in these circumstances.

Synthetic Parallelism

He established	the earth	on its foundations
It shall not be moved	forever	and ever.

Psalm 104:5

(See Henry Neufeld's paper on Psalm 104 for the differences in this text and more standard translations.)[12]

Synthetic parallelism can be interpreted much like prose. The second portion expands on the same topic, and uses the same meter (again, I'm not discussing meter as it is less important for interpretation), but does not have a defined relationship to the previous line element by element.

We are skipping climactic parallelism, in which the second and/or third lines produce a climax, often being parallel in one element, but adding more in building to a climax. It is identical to synthetic parallelism in terms of interpretation, except that you may find a closer relationship between the meaning of the lines of poetry.

---

12 Henry E. Neufeld, Psalm 104: God – Creator and Sustainer, http://rpp. energion.com/psalm104.shtml, accessed February 23, 2010.

One more characteristic of Hebrew poetry that should be mentioned, though it won't impact interpretation very much, is the acrostic. Psalm 119 is an excellent example, in with 176 verses are divided into 22 sections of 8 verses each, and in each section every verse begins with the same letter of the Hebrew alphabet. The sections are sequential, so that one completes the Hebrew alphabet with all verses in the last section starting with the last letter (tau). When interpreting Psalm 119, you should remember that this form has much more to do with the arrangement of the verses than does the topic of each verse. To read Psalm 119 topically, you need to read scattered verses that use the same key words wherever they occur in the psalm.

You can find much more information on the various types of Hebrew poetry, and some discussion of meter in a good Bible dictionary or Old Testament introduction.[13]

These labels for the types of parallelism are not necessarily precise. You will find lines of poetry that combine the various types. In addition, many of the more dynamic translations, such as the CEV do not translate the parallelism, instead constructing a single statement from the parts of the parallelism that gives the meaning.

Types of Psalms and other Poetry

The major types are:

- **Hymn**
  Example: Psalm 104. Sometimes Psalm 104 is also considered wisdom literature due to references to wisdom and creation and parallels to Proverbs 8 and 9.
- **Prayers**
  Luke 2:29-21 (the Song of Simeon), Psalm 3 (Prayer for Deliverance)

---

13   There is an excellent article in the *New Oxford Annotated Bible* (ISBN: 0-19-528356-2), titled *Characteristics of Hebrew Poetry*, page 392.

- **Thanksgiving**
  Psalm 118
- **Petition**
  Psalm 22 (often petitions can also be classified as laments
- **Confession**
  Psalm 51
- **Lament**
  Extensively throughout the book of Lamentations, Psalm 22.
- **Wisdom and/or Teaching**
  Psalm 78
- **Song of Celebration**
  Judges 5
- **Prophetic Oracle**
  Isaiah 14:3-21
- **Proverb or Common Saying**
  Proverbs 10:7 and many more in the same book

Exercise

Choose one of the following passages and find various types of parallelism in the Hebrew poetry:

1. Psalm 104

2. Psalm 29

3. Psalm 137

4. Proverbs 9

5. Isaiah 55

You may also want to write your own poetic reflection on a Psalm. Use some of the techniques of Hebrew poetry and integrate them with modern poetic techniques.

Here's an example from Henry Neufeld's fiction and poetry blog, The Jevlir Caravansary, Psalm 46 as an Italian Sonnet[14]:

I'm safe with God my strength, my shield, my friend.
In danger he is sure and will be there.
When broken world and shattered mount I dare,
No fear I know, on God I will depend.

All water's safe where God his help can lend.
His city glows with joy as streams there fare.
The center of his city's in his care.
At dawn he comes, he shouts, he will defend.

My God is here with troops, his joy, his strength.
Let's look and see what works he's going to show.
He stops a war, he goes and weapons breaks.

Be quiet, soul, the world watch, breadth and length
See how all know he's great wher'ere winds blow.
He rules, he saves, he hears, all peace he makes.

---

14 Henry Neufeld, Psalm 46 as an Italian Sonnet, http://www.jevlir.com/?
   p=9, accessed February 23, 2010.

14

Letters

Learning how the experience of reading someone else's mail — the many epistles or letters in the Bible — impacts our understanding

We use the term "letter," because that is the common modern term. In church sometimes they are also called epistles. Letters focus on getting some message to a particular group. They may contain other types of literature within them.

You may be surprised at how much of the New Testament consists of letters. The material in this section applies to interpreting the following Bible books:

- **Pauline Epistles to Churches**
  - Romans
  - 1 Corinthians
  - 2 Corinthians
  - Galatians
  - Ephesians
  - Philippians
  - Colossians
  - 1 Thessalonians
  - 2 Thessalonians
- **Pastoral Epistles**
  - 1 Timothy
  - 2 Timothy
  - Titus
  - Philemon
- **General Epistles**
  - Hebrews

- James
- 1 Peter
- 2 Peter
- 1 John
- 2 John
- 3 John
- Jude

Epistles are simply letters written by some of the early church leaders to people under their spiritual care. We hesitate to use the term "pastor" to refer only to the letters to Timothy and Titus, because all of these letters result from a pastoral concern. The focus is on responding to, or anticipating, certain problems in the church and providing guidance for those situations. In some cases this guidance is in the form of correction or rebuke; in others it is in the form of encouragement. Sometimes passages explain certain doctrinal issues.

None of the Bible is written primarily as theology, though some things come close. Most Christian theology is built primarily around statements in the epistles, especially the epistles of Paul. Hebrews (for those who do not accept Pauline authorship) comes in a close second. But even when we are dealing with the theological passages in these epistles, we should remember that the writer is responding to practical issues in the life of the church. In other words, the doctrines presented or explained are those doctrines the churches or individuals need to understand in order to effectively live the Christian life.

It is important in reading those portions of the epistles in which the author is making theological or doctrinal arguments, for the reader to be careful to read precisely what is there. For help in this process, see the earlier section on reading precisely (p. 34).

Key Questions about Background

The key questions you want to ask about the background of an epistle are:

- Who wrote it?
- Who was it written to?
- What were the circumstances under which it was written? A letter can be a response to a particular situation or it can be simply a newsy update. It is often important to know what questions are being asked if one is to understand the answers. In particular, Paul has clearly received some questions from the church in Corinth, and he responds in the letter we call 1 Corinthians. Trying to understand what question he must be answering may help you understand the answers he is giving.
- When was it written?
  This is for broader background. When we understand the immediate circumstances, we have most of what we need to understand the letter. But knowing the date of the letter can help us answer both those questions, and tell us something of where the broader church was at the time of the letter.

In the Central Loop

See Chapter 7: The Central Loop for a description of the central loop.

In studying epistles, you will find the greatest use for skills such as word studies, detailed outlining, and for Greek students, diagramming, and detailed parsing (studying the forms) of particular words. This is because when we are trying to understand logical (or sometimes not so logical) arguments, we need to get a precise understanding of each word, its relationship to the phrase, and that to the sentence, paragraph, and the entire subsection of the letter.

Most inductive Bible study methods are focused on precisely this type of study. But you can also get much more from a letter by looking at it somewhat like a piece of a story. Around that one piece, you will build the rest of the story. Who wrote it? Why?

Who was he writing to? In understanding the letter and getting a feel for the story behind it, your imagination will play a key role. Don't be afraid to try to imagine these other elements.

Besides the standard set of ideas from the central loop, we suggest some specific exercises below that apply to letters.

Exercise

1. Make a Comparison Chart for the Letter's Recipients

This chart is written for 1 Corinthians, but you can make a list of the characteristics of the audience for whatever epistle you choose to read.

Corinthian Church	Your Church	Solution?
Divided into factions		
Problem with spiritual pride		
Sexual immorality		
Disorderly worship services		
Doctrinal drift		

Try to be honest in looking at your church. Don't pretend it's worse than it is, but do recognize your own faults as well as those of your church. Try then to use your strengths as a starting point to build up your church and overcome your weaknesses. Most of the epistles are written to churches, groups of churches or church leaders. You will generally find that there is something, usually many things, that are relevant to your situation.

Letters are a wonderful option for group study and discussion, especially when a cross-section of church leadership participates.

2. Imagine that you are one of the recipients, and write a reply. If you are studying as an individual, you may decide just to write out the main points. In group discussion, ask for points from the group, and write them on a dry erase board. You don't need to get wordy in the letter, but try to get both the points you would make, and the tone in which you would make them. Then ask why.

3. Write a letter based on the same themes to your own church, as though it comes from the author of the letter. Again, if you are studying individually you may want to write a point outline. In a group, outline both the points and the tone, and think about the priority. Supposing you only had space to make three points, which would they be (think of having to present the letter on one page or on a small airmail letter)? What if you could only make one, and that one on a postcard? What would it be?

15

Prophecy

Focusing on the key to prophesy –
bringing God's message to particular times and circumstances.

In Biblical terms, prophecy is simply speaking for God, a person presenting a message that he or she has received from God. In modern times, the term *prophecy* has become closely connected with prediction, and specifically with predicting events that deal with the end times and the second coming of Jesus. But the predictive element, and particularly the end times element, is actually a rather small portion of what prophecy is in the Bible.

For purposes of this chapter, we're going to ignore those areas in which someone writes a story under divine inspiration, or a book of history. In a sense, Luke is speaking for God (prophesying) when he writes his gospel, but that is not the same thing as we might say of Hosea, Jeremiah, Ezekiel, or Isaiah. The prophets are people that announce the reign of God. Their message is usually social and political in nature. They layout a vision of God's plan for the world in stark contrast to way we have caused thew world to be. The prophets often go head to head with kings and rulers on God's behalf.

Prophecy and Prediction

Is there an element of prediction in prophecy? Certainly there is! Where interpreters and Bible students tend to get into trouble is when they assume that the prediction is the major element in the words spoken by the prophet.

Let's consider the book of Jonah. Jonah is called to give a message to Nineveh, one that he wants to avoid giving. Often we get distracted from the meaning of the book right here. The issue of the storm at sea and the whale is simply a narrative element designed to move Jonah unwillingly toward God's goal. At this point in the story we should be looking at the reasons Jonah is so anxious not to present the message. If Jonah thought that he was presenting a simple prediction of the future, would he not enjoy going to Nineveh, telling the Ninevites that their lives were over, and then watching until his prediction came true? But he runs away. In Jonah 4:2 he tells us why: He was afraid God would be merciful, and thus his prediction would not come true.

This highlights a difference between Jonah's view of the situation and God's view. God is not predicting a future event that he knows will happen. Instead, God is telling someone, in this case the Ninevites, what he is going to do. When God does this, his intention is to give them the option to do something about the problem that was coming. The Ninevites are told that in 40 days their city will be destroyed. They repent and it does not happen. This highlights the purpose of prophecy: Changing people!

Note that the book of Jonah can also be interpreted as story. In fact, that is what we are doing here, interpreting the story in order to give us a better understanding of prophecy.

Alden Thompson, in lecturing on the topic, refers to this as a "failed prediction, successful prophecy."[15] In our eyes, a prophecy fails when the event predicted does not happen. In God's eyes, the prophecy quite often fails when it *does* come true.

Are we building too much theology on this story, one which some scholars think is simply a fictional story built around the historical character of Jonah? Let's look at another passage:

---

15 Alden Thompson, www.AldenThompson.com, accessed February 23, 2010.

> When at a certain time I speak concerning a nation,
> To uproot, tear down, and destroy
> And that nation turns from its evil,
> About which I spoke.
> Then I will repent of the evil I intended to do to it
> But if at a certain time I speak concerning a nation,
> To build and to plant,
> And that nation does evil in my eyes
> And doesn't obey my voice
> Then I will repent of the good that I said I would
> do to it. — *Jeremiah 18:7-10*

So here we are explicitly told that God's intent is to change the way people behave, and if they do, he will change what it is that he was planning to do.

How does this relate to the test of a prophet in Deuteronomy 18:21-22? Here is where Christians have generally gotten the idea that every prediction must, in fact, come true, despite Jeremiah's statement to the contrary. Yet, Deuteronomy states that the prophecy must take place or prove true. Thus, when we look at the prophecy, we must ask whether God accomplished his intention with the prediction, and not simply at whether the event predicted took place.

Let's compare this to a parent dealing with a child. The parent promises the child an ice cream cone if he behaves well. The child does not behave well, and when the time comes, the parent fails to buy the ice cream cone. The child is angry! The parent has broken a promise! Yet the condition was there. In parenting, we even have the situation of an unstated condition. If a child asks to go somewhere special, the parent might say yes. Nonetheless, if the child's behavior changes, even though the condition was not explicitly stated, permission might be withdrawn as punishment. A promise can be conditional even when that is not stated.

Questions to Ask about a Prophecy

In studying a prophecy, you need to ask the basic questions of context: When was the prophecy given? Who was the prophet? For whom was the prophecy intended?

But you must then also ask what the purpose of the prophecy was. What is the result that God is trying to produce with this prophecy? The answer to that question will help you understand how to apply the prophecy appropriately.

Prophetic Language

There are several characteristics of prophetic language that require special attention when interpreting prophecy. These are:

- Poetic language
- Hyperbole and sweeping language
- Symbolic language
- Vision and dream descriptions

Poetic Language

Much of the prophecy that we have in written form is presented as poetry. Poetry as a literary form tends to force the way that the message is presented into certain channels demanded by the poetic style. You need to be aware of this form in interpretation. For example, Hebrew poetry uses parallelism. This feature uses parallel terms in succeeding lines of text that might be synonyms, antonyms, or they might be complementary. In addition, some elements might be left out in the text, and the meaning is to be taken from the parallel line.

Consider this example:

| A lamp | for my feet | [is] your word |
| And a light | for my path | --- |

The words "lamp" and "light" are parallel, as are "feet" and "path." We fill in the subject of the second line as "your word" according to the parallel. Such combined lines generally combine to present a single truth, rather than presenting separate points.

For more information on interpreting poetry, see Chapter 13: Poetry.

Hyperbole and Sweeping Language

The prophets tended to talk in large terms. Sometimes this results in an appearance of falsehood. Some interpreters will try to apply single verses or short passages to some other situation because of this language, but this is no more than a feature of the type of language involved. After a recent hurricane passed through my hometown, I made the comment that there was destruction everywhere, that some areas looked like a giant had stepped on them. Now one would hardly hold me to the true definition of "everywhere." To do so would be to expect of me the precision of a scientific report rather than a personal exclamation. Neither would one expect the area to look precisely like it would if a giant had, in fact, stepped on it. Both of these are hyperbolic statements.

Now let's consider an example, Jeremiah 4 has a prediction of the invasion and destruction of Judah at the time of the Babylonian exile. From verse 1 to verse 22 the language is quite clear, though it is poetic. Starting with verse 23, it becomes hyperbolic.

> I looked at the land, and it was wasted and empty
> And to the heavens, but there was no light. I looked
> at the mountains and they were shaking, And the
> hills and they were moving back and forth. I
> looked, and there were no human beings, And
> every bird of the heavens had fled.

Because of key elements such as "everything empty," "no human beings," and "no light," many see this short passage of poetry as describing some other event of judgment. Judah was not totally destroyed as these words might imply. But if we look at the end of verse 27, the prophet continues, speaking for God, "but even so I will not make an end of all the land." In other words, reports of the land being totally empty are, perhaps, a bit exaggerated. Or are they? That may be precisely what the prophet saw in vision. Yet by the context it is still part of the judgment on Judah.

We must remember that God is not just speaking generally; God is speaking to specific people about a specific situation. It is unjustified to suddenly assume that he started to talk about something completely different without any warning. In fact, understanding the hyperbolic language allows us to see this as a unified, rational passage, and to interpret it in its own context.

Symbolic Language

Prophets use symbolic and allegorical language. A good example of allegorical language can be found in Ezekiel 16 (see Chapter 12: Parables and Allegory). Symbolic language occurs especially in the language of vision, and most especially in apocalyptic visions such as those in Daniel and Revelation. Nonetheless one can find symbolic language in many other passages as well. For example, in Isaiah 27:1 we have God's judgment on Leviathan, probably representing evil. In Isaiah 55, we have water, wine, milk, and bread all used as symbols for spiritual blessings that the Lord is prepared to provide.

There are two tools that are most useful when attempting to understand symbolic language: A concordance and a Bible Dictionary. In the concordance you look for all other instances of the use of that symbol in the Bible. Remember, however, that a symbol is not necessarily used in only one way. A Bible dictionary will give you definitions, and generally will also point you to the most important references. The final way to determine the meaning is by its immediate context.

Conclusion

Prophecy requires some special care in interpretation, but in the end, it is simply another way in which God communicates with us. We look for God's message for us as we look at how he communicated with others in ancient times.

Exercises

1. Read Jeremiah 4. What examples do you find of hyperbolic language? Is there a reason this chapter is written in poetic language?

2. Isaiah 55 is a prophetic passage. What, if anything, is predicted in this passage? What is the purpose of the message? To whom is it addressed?

16

Visions and Dreams

Looking at the visions and dreams that are found throughout scripture and learning to understand them.

This chapter deals specifically with how to interpret visions. It builds on material in *Chapter 15: Interpreting Prophecy*, which should be read first.

Prophetic Visions and Dreams in the Bible

There are quite a number of instances of prophetic visions and dreams in the Bible, though they are heavily concentrated in Daniel, Zechariah, Revelation, and also scattered through the various prophetic books. Isaiah and Ezekiel, for example, give particularly vivid reports of visions.

Some of the visions and dreams and their major message are included in the following table:

Vision or Dream	Passage	Note
Abimelech's Dream	Genesis 20:3-7	Abimelech is given information verbally in the dream. No symbolism is used.
Jacob's Ladder Dream	Genesis 28:12-17	The ladder to heaven with angels on it, though most information is in the words spoken.

Vision or Dream	Passage	Note
Jacob and Laban's Guidance Dreams	Genesis 31:10-24	These are very interesting as part of the conflict between these two manipulative men.
Joseph's First Two Dreams	Genesis 37:5-11	The symbolism is quite clear in these dreams.
The Baker and Butler's Dream	Genesis 40:5-8	The interpretations are presented by Joseph.
Pharaoh's Dreams	Genesis 41	The interpretations are presented by Joseph.
Solomon's Dream	1 Kings 3:5-9	This was a response to a prayer
Nebuchadnezzar's Dream of the Image	Daniel 2	Daniel interprets
Nebuchadnezzar's Dream of a Tree	Daniel 4	Daniel interprets
Daniel's Dream of 4 Beasts	Daniel 7	Interpretation follows dream
Joseph's Dream	Matthew 1:20	Fairly simple and straightforward
Pilate's Wife's Dream	Matthew 27:19	We are given the interpretation but not the form of the dream
Abraham's 2nd Call Vision	Genesis 15	An important vision for the history of Israel
Isaiah's Call	Isaiah 6	Prophetic call
Ezekiel's Call	Ezekiel 1	Prophetic call
Temple Judgment	Ezekiel 8-10	Part of the extended series

Vision or Dream	Passage	Note
		of visions in Ezekiel about the glory of God
Dry Bones	Ezekiel 37	One of the most famous visions in scripture
Temple Vision	Ezekiel 40-48	Ezekiel sees a new temple; an excellent study of symbolic language.
Daniel's Visions	Daniel 8-12	After the initial dream of Daniel 7, Daniel has several further visions.
Eight Visions	Zechariah 1-6	The first part of Zechariah is almost all visionary.
Man from Macedonia	Acts 16:9-10	Paul is told given a call to a new mission in a vision.
Revelation	Entire Book	Entire book probably consists of a single vision

The Vision State

When I was in undergraduate study, I chose to do research on Ezekiel's vision in the first chapter. One of the things I became convinced of was that much of the difficulty in understanding that chapter resulted from Ezekiel writing it under the influence of a vision. He was not able to think of the precise wording to use, and so he described things multiple times, and sometimes repeated himself and seemed confused. Some commentators have even gone to the effort to try and clean out the first chapter of things that they feel are the result of textual corruption. It is these elements that I believe are part of the vision state.

After my study, I tried several times to present my understanding of Ezekiel 1 to various audiences, spending at least a couple of hours on each occasion, but I had only partial success. Then I had the opportunity to present the same material to a group of students who had experienced the Pensacola Outpouring (Brownsville Revival, Pensacola, Florida, 1995-2000). Each of them had either experienced a vision or spiritual dream or at least knew someone who did. Experiencing visions and dreams are common in the Charismatic or Pentecostal movement. Within 20 minutes, I saw looks of comprehension on their faces, and soon they were discussing the chapter in some detail. They understood the excitement of having a vision, and the difficulty of explaining what you see to another person.

You can see a similar phenomenon in Revelation, as John finds it difficult to describe what he sees. Look especially at the vision of Jesus in the first chapter, where John uses the word 'like' as he struggles to find a word to describe the Christ he sees.

Remember two things as you interpret visions and dreams: 1) The language used in describing the vision may be imprecise, and may change, and 2) The vision description may not be entirely logical or sequential, and may also not be chronological. It is probably arranged visually, and not according to another logical scheme. Look for the tie-ins between scenes in the vision, and look for multiple descriptions, and combine them in trying to understand what it is that the prophet sees.

Conclusion

Visions and dreams present the same type of information, and generally have the same purpose as prophecy, but the information is presented in an other way.

Exercise

Choose any of the vision passages list in the chart on page 101. Answer the following questions:

1. Why is God's message in this passage presented as a vision?

2. What is the key point of the vision?

3. What did the prophet actually see in this vision?

4. How might the message have been understood or felt if it had been presented in another way, for example in simple prose?

17

Wisdom

*Wisdom literature brings us the wisdom
from many centuries of life as God's people*

Basics

The Biblical wisdom literature takes a different approach to knowledge of God than do either the prophetic or the historical books. In the books of history, we are presented with an interpretation of God's actions in the history of the community and what that says about God and his relationship to the world. The prophetic books instead claim to present a message *from* God, that is we get God's message as it was presented at a particular time and place.

The approach of wisdom literature is somewhat different. It reflects the experience both of the community and of the individual provided through years of experience and reflection. Wisdom still comes from God, in the wisdom books no less than in any other Biblical literature, but the process is one of education, reflection, and growth.

For example, at the beginning of Ecclesiastes we read:

> I, Qoheleth, was king over Israel in Jerusalem. I applied my mind to seek and to discover wisdom about everything that is done under the heavens, what a nasty business it is that God has given human beings with which to be occupied. – *Ecclesiastes 1:12-13*

This passage comes near the beginning of the book, in about the position we might expect to find the prophetic call, and the statement that a prophetic writer was getting his message from God. It is clear from wisdom literature that the ultimate source is God, as can be seen even in the two verses I quoted, but experience and reflection are much more important components here.

Look also at Proverbs 1:1-6 and notice words like instruction, teach, learning, acquiring skill, and so forth. But none of this changes the ultimate #1 rule: "The fear of YHWH (the LORD) is the beginning of knowledge; fools despise wisdom and instruction." – *Proverbs 1:7*

Wisdom books are thus asking you to learn from the collected experience of the community and of acknowledged people of wisdom. In addition, it builds most clearly the connection between God's creation and our learning from it (Proverbs 8:22-31; Psalm 19; Psalm 104).

You will find wisdom literature primarily in Ecclesiastes, Proverbs, and Job, but you will also find examples scattered through the Bible, especially in the Psalms.

Proverbs

Proverbs provide some special problems for interpretation. A proverb is a short, pithy saying that conveys some general truth. The key here is *short*. While you can expect many miracles in the inspiration of the Bible, there is no miracle performed to make a short saying convey the same information as a long one.

Because of this, there are some keys to using proverbs:

1. Look for a single central message. A proverb is generally intended to make one point.
2. Don't expect the proverb to be applicable in all circumstances. One thing that allows a proverb to be

short is the omission of the details of circumstances and
all the exceptions.
3. Be sure you hear precisely what the proverb says. There
is very little context to help you correct your understanding.

Compare the following two proverbs in the English language:

Too many cooks spoil the broth.

Many hands make light work.

They appear contradictory, don't they? But can you think of
times when either one would be applicable, but of course not the
other?

Now look at Proverbs 26:4-5:

Don't answer a fool according to his foolishness,
lest you become a fool yourself just like him.

Answer a fool according to his foolishness,
Lest he become wise in his own eyes.

Aha! A contradiction in the Bible!

But wait! These are proverbs, and they are not intended to apply
universally. Can you think of circumstances in which each of
these proverbs might apply? Sometimes someone is speaking
foolishly, and all that is necessary is for somebody to point this
out, preventing others from being led astray, and sometimes
even correcting the foolish individual. At other times, someone
may confuse a willingness to debate with them as respect for
their position. Which one do you use in any particular
circumstances? That's what *wisdom* is about!

We like the metaphor of the toolkit here. We could get hung up
on the apparent contradiction between these two verses, but
instead, we can look at each verse as a tool. In construction,

when you need to cut a specific size piece out of a board, you need a saw. Now when you go to your toolkit, and see there a hammer and a saw, you don't discard the toolkit because it is inconsistent. You don't discard the hammer because it is not necessary. Rather, you select the saw, because it is applicable to your situation at the moment.

Similarly Jesus, in talking about forgiveness, gave a set of tools, not a single answer. In Matthew 18:15-20, he gave instructions for reproving a brother who sins against you, including going to the congregation to get a judgment. But then in Matthew 18:21-22, he essentially demands endless forgiveness, with no mention of reproof. Depending on what translation you're using, the instruction is to forgive either 77 times or 490 times. In either case, if you've kept count up to that number of times, there's something really weak about your forgiveness!

Thus a study of proverbs can help us understand the rest of the Bible. We develop wisdom to determine when the process of reproof is the best to apply to a situation, and when absolute and simple forgiveness is the correct response. This shows us again why we cannot ignore any portion of the Bible.

Ecclesiastes

Ecclesiastes has given interpreters a great deal of difficulty. Many people try to alleviate its apparent cynicism by some very creative ways of interpreting. But all of these schemes tend to play games with the actual text of the book. It was clearly written by a discouraged man.

It will help to recognize what we said in the introduction to this chapter. Wisdom literature is about the process of learning, of how we come to understanding. While it is argued whether Solomon had anything to do with writing the book, it is clear that his experience is in view. Ask yourself this: How would *you* write if you had spent your life like Solomon did, come to the end of it, and realized things were about to fall apart (the kingdom split right after Solomon's death), and that you had wasted your life, in spite of having the ability to live wisely?

In the Bible, God has given us many experiences that we can place alongside our own experience to come to better understand how we can relate to God in all circumstances. Ecclesiastes is one of those books; difficult, but very encouraging in the right time and place.

Exercise

1. Choose a random section of five or six verses from Proverbs, preferably from the later chapters (10 or later). Try to imagine a situation in which each of the proverbs applies, and another one in which it does not.
2. Read Proverbs 8 & 9. What is the role of personified wisdom in creation?
3. How might your life story differ if you told it at your moment of greatest discouragement? At a moment of triumph?
4. What problems can you see with community wisdom or learning from tradition? What benefits?

Glossary

This glossary defines a limited number of terms that are used without adequate explanation in the text. We have not included words that are explained as they are introduced.

Allegory – a story in which various elements represent something other than what they reference literally.

American Standard Version – A Bible translation from the turn of the 19th to the 20th century. It updated some language from the King James Version, but the language is still somewhat archaic today. It formed the foundation for the New American Standard Bible.

Chronology – the study of when events took place in the Bible, and how this relates to events in the surrounding countries.

Client State – a state that is dependent on another one either economically or politically for it's existence.

English Revised Version – the 1888 revision of the King James Version. It is a bit wooden in style and the language is now quite archaic.

Epistle – a letter, used of the Bible books written as letters to various people and churches.

Formal Equivalence – a style of translation in which the translator tries to match each word or word form in the source language with a single word or phrase in the target language. While it provides consistent wording that helps in concordance study, the language will often not sound natural.

Functional Equivalence – a style of translation in which the translator tries to match the function or the impact of the text in the original language in translation. It normally results in translations that sound more natural and are easier to read.

King James Version – a respected achievement in Bible translation from 1611 AD. It is still in print and advocated by some. We do not recommend it for your Bible study due to archaic language and the many new discoveries in texts and language that have been made since it was produced.

Parable – a story usually intended to convey a single point.

Topical Index

Scripture Index

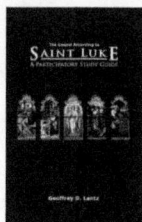

The Gospel According to Saint Luke: A Participatory Study Guide by Geoffrey Lentz

Geoffrey Lentz provides a new look at the gospel of Luke for small groups that is thoughtful, practical, and with a strong emphasis on prayer and meditation. If you want to learn and live this important gospel, this is the study guide for you!

To the Hebrews: A Participatory Study Guide by Henry Neufeld

The book of Hebrews provides a unique view of the ministry of Jesus as Redeemer, priest, sacrifice, and king. Learn to live as a redeemed person through this powerful New Testament book, guided by a thematic study guide that invites you deeper into the book with each lesson.

Revelation: A Participatory Study Guide by Henry Neufeld

Built around the metaphor of a theme park ride, inspired by *The Pirates of the Caribbean*, this study guide takes a visual approach to Revelation. It's not about dates and charts. It's not just about the future. It's about you and how you are going to live a Christian life in this world, but not of it.

Coming April, 2010 …

The Character of Our Discontent: Old Testament Portraits for Contemporary Times by Dr. Allan R. Bevere

The Character of Our Discontent grew out of the author's conviction that pastors do not preach enough about the Old Testament. The result is 19 chapters, each of which represents a sermon on an Old Testament character. These sermons are lively, fast paced, and practical yet are rooted in sound scholarship and are examples of the homiletical art.

Allan R. Bevere is the pastor of First United Methodist Church in Cambridge, Ohio and a Professional Fellow in Theology at Ashland Theological Seminary in Ashland, Ohio. He received his Ph.D from the University of Durham, U.K.

To order, visit any major online retailer, or see our web site at:

EnergionDirect.com
http://www.energiondirect.com

Phone: (850) 525-3916
P. O. Box 841
Gonzalez, FL 32560

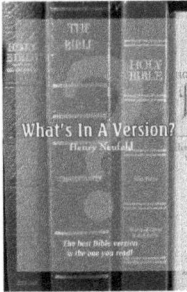

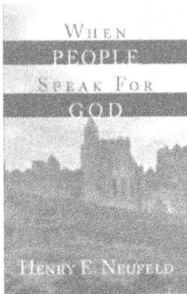

More from Energion Publications

Personal Study

The Jesus Paradigm	$17.99
When People Speak for God	$17.99
Holy Smoke, Unholy Fire	$14.99
Not Ashamed of the Gospel	$12.99
Evidence for the Bible	$16.99
Christianity and Secularism	$16.99
What's In A Version?	$12.99
Christian Archy	$9.99
The Messiah and His Kingdom to Come: A Biblical Road Map	$19.99 (B&W)
(an EnerPower Press title)	$49.99 (Color)

Christian Living

52 Weeks of Ordinary People – Extraordinary God	$7.99
Daily Devotions of Ordinary People – Extraordinary God	$19.99
Directed Paths	$7.99
Grief: Finding the Candle of Light	$8.99
I Want to Pray	$7.99

Bible Study for Groups

To the Hebrews: A Participatory Study Guide	$9.99
Revelation: A Participatory Study Guide	$9.99
The Gospel According to St. Luke: A Participatory Study Guide	$8.99
Identifying Your Gifts and Service: Small Group Edition	$12.99
Consider Christianity, Volume I & II Study Guides	$7.99 each

Politics

Preserving Democracy (Hardcover)	$29.99

Fiction

Tales from Jevlir: Oddballs	$7.99
(an Enzar Empire Press title)	
Megabelt	$12.99

Generous Quantity Discounts Available
Dealer Inquiries Welcome

Energion Publications
P.O. Box 841
Gonzalez, FL 32560
Website: http://energionpubs.com
Email: pubs@energion.com
Phone: (850) 525-3916